Peacock Books

Best Science Fiction of the

'I was at the spaceport an ho
clone-sister was to arrive fro
eagerness to see her. She was three E-years
and we had never met . . . I've never been off-planet. Someday I'll go, but not as a paying passenger. I was about to enrol in pilot-training school.'

So John Varley begins his 'Retrograde Summer,' a vivid and fascinating story of life on a Mercury colony – one of the best science fiction stories published in 1975 by such authors as Harlan Ellison, Gregory Benford, Algis Budrys and Gene Wolfe, chosen by Terry Carr. In each story we are introduced to a world of the future, and we see how it came to be and why. Each has its own excitement and sense of wonder. As Terry Carr says in his introduction, 'Be prepared for anything in these pages . . . and you'll still be surprised!'

Publisher's Note

The other stories selected for *Best Science Fiction of the Year 1* are published in a companion volume (Part Two).

Best Science Fiction of the Year - 1

PART ONE

Edited by Terry Carr

Peacock Books

Penguin Books Ltd, Harmondsworth,
Middlesex, England
Penguin Books, 625 Madison Avenue,
New York, New York 10022, U.S.A.
Penguin Books Australia Ltd, Ringwood,
Victoria, Australia
Penguin Books Canada Ltd, 2801 John Street,
Markham, Ontario, Canada L3R 1B4
Penguin Books (N.Z.) Ltd, 182–190 Wairau Road,
Auckland 10, New Zealand

First published in *Best Science Fiction of the Year 5*
by Victor Gollancz Ltd 1976

Published with a new Introduction as *Best Science Fiction of the Year 1 – Part One* in Peacock Books 1978

Made and printed in Great Britain by
C. Nicholls & Company Ltd
Set in Linotype Juliana

Contents

Acknowledgements 7

Introduction *Terry Carr* 9

Down to a Sunless Sea *Cordwainer Smith* 13

Retrograde Summer *John Varley* 49

The Hero as Werwolf *Gene Wolfe* 75

The Silent Eyes of Time *Algis Budrys* 95

Croatoan *Harlan Ellison* 154

Doing Lennon *Gregory Benford* 171

Recommended Reading – 1975 187

Acknowledgements

DOWN TO A SUNLESS SEA by Cordwainer Smith. Copyright © 1975 by Mercury Press, Inc. From *Fantasy and Science Fiction*, October 1975, by permission of the author and his agents, Scott Meredith Literary Agency, Inc.

RETROGRADE SUMMER by John Varley. Copyright © 1975 by Mercury Press, Inc.; copyright reassigned to the author. From *Fantasy and Science Fiction*, February 1975, by permission of the author.

THE HERO AS WERWOLF by Gene Wolfe. Copyright © 1975 by Thomas Disch. From *The New Improved Sun*, by permission of the author and his agent, Virginia Kidd.

THE SILENT EYES OF TIME by Algis Budrys. Copyright © 1975 by Mercury Press, Inc. From *Fantasy and Science Fiction*, November 1975, by permission of the author and his agents, Candida Donadio and Associates, Inc.

CROATOAN by Harlan Ellison. Copyright © 1975 by Harlan Ellison. From *Fantasy and Science Fiction*, May 1975, by permission of the author and the author's agent, Robert P. Mills, Ltd.

DOING LENNON by Gregory Benford. Copyright © 1975 by The Condé Nast Publications Inc. From *Analog*, April 1975, by permission of the author.

Introduction

Science fiction today is both an enormously popular field of entertainment and one regarded with respect by people in high places. Courses in science fiction are taught in hundreds of universities, science fiction writers are compared to literary masters like Joseph Conrad and Charles Dickens, and their speculations about the future are solicited by executives of giant corporations looking for tips on supply and marketing possibilities to come.

It wasn't always like this. Only a few years ago, most people thought of science fiction as 'crazy' or unbelievable, or at best as a diverting type of story without relevance to the *real* world. But today we live in a world that has seen space travel, atomic power, television and myriad other science-fiction notions become accepted facts; the passage of time has brought vindication to the science fiction writers who wrote of these things forty or fifty years ago.

In view of such widespread acceptance and interest, science fiction authors and readers find it tempting to think of these stories about the future as being just the same as 'ordinary' literature. But science fiction *isn't* exactly like other forms of fiction; it's something new, a way of looking at the world that offers different qualities.

Basically, science fiction deals in ideas, and what long-time readers call the 'sense of wonder', a feeling of strangeness and awe at the vast scope of future history. Conventional fiction does just the opposite: its stock-in-trade is a feeling of easy recognition of settings and events from today's world.

Compare, for instance, the grand, large-scale ideas of Isaac Asimov's *Foundation* or Larry Niven's *Tales of Known Space* with the kinds of things that have most often been praised in traditional literature: Jane Austen commenting on the nuances of a character's expression, or J. D. Salinger cataloguing the contents of the Glass family's medicine cabinet.

Traditionally, literature has dealt in such specificity, telling stories that seem so real we can *feel* the 'meanings' in them. Science fiction is usually more direct: characters *talk* about the ideas in their stories, and sometimes fight interstellar wars over them.

This is, in part, the result of necessity – for it's very difficult to explain the workings of a galactic empire by listing a star-lord's deodorants and washcloths: You have to be able to see how a future world works before you can understand it, so science fiction writers have to tell you much more about their imagined worlds.

But in this lies the fascination of science fiction, for in each story you see a new world, and how it came to be, and why. As you come to understand these worlds, you may feel pure delight, as in John Varley's picture of a colony on Mercury in 'Retrograde Summer', or fear like that in Gene Wolfe's 'The Hero as Werwolf', or the kind of exaltation in the fliers' world of Tuttle and Martin's 'The Storms of Windhaven' (see Part II).

Each story, though, presents a new world for you to explore, and each has its own excitement.

The stories in this book are the cream of the crop from an entire year of science fiction, the best from hundreds of stories published in magazines and books by the most imaginative writers in the world. They present a kaleidoscope of newness : strange ideas, unfamiliar experiences.

Be prepared for anything in these pages . . . and you'll still be surprised.

Terry Carr
Oakland, June 1977

Down to a Sunless Sea

Cordwainer Smith

When Cordwainer Smith's first story, 'Scanners Live in Vain', appeared in an obscure magazine called Fantasy Book *in 1950, the editor hailed it as 'one of the most outstanding stories to appear in any magazine', and time has confirmed his judgement: 'Scanners' became recognized as a classic of science fiction, and it launched one of the most remarkable careers in this field. As story after story appeared under the Smith byline, each contributing to a 'future history' of unprecedented originality, readers became more and more curious about who might be hiding behind this obvious pseudonym. After many years the secret came out: 'Cordwainer Smith' was Dr Paul M. A. Linebarger, an American who was a godson of Sun Yat Sen, an Army Intelligence officer in China during World War II, later an adviser to President Kennedy and Professor of Asiatic Politics at the Johns Hopkins University.*

Dr Linebarger died in 1966, and since then we've had no new 'Smith' stories – till the following delightful novelette appeared last year. Begun by Dr Linebarger, it was completed by his widow, Genevieve, who had collaborated with him on some earlier stories. Members of the growing legions of 'Smith' fans will find this latest tale as colourful and fascinating as all the stories of the Lords of the Instrumentality, the Underpeople and the rest of the strange inhabitants of Cordwainer Smith's imagined future.

HIGH OH, HIGH *oh, they jingle in the sky oh! Bright how bright the light of those twin moons of Xanadu, Xanadu the lost, Xanadu the lovely, Xanadu the seat of pleasure. Pleasure of the senses, body, mind, soul. Soul? Who said anything about soul?*

I

Where they were standing the wind whispered softly. From time to time Madu in an ageless feminine gesture tugged at her tiny silver skirt or adjusted her equally nominal open sleeveless jacket. Not that she was cold. Her abbreviated costume was appropriate to Xanadu's equable climate.

She thought: 'I wonder what he will be like, this Lord of the Instrumentality? Will he be old or young, fair or dark, wise or foolish?' She did not think 'handsome or ugly'. Xanadu was noted for the physical perfection of its inhabitants, and Madu was too young to expect anything less.

Lari, waiting beside her, was not thinking of the Space Lord. His mind was seeing again the video tapes of the dancing, the intricate steps and beautiful frenzy of movement of the group from ancient days on Manhome, the group labelled 'Bawlshoy'. 'Someday,' he thought, 'oh, perhaps someday I too can dance like that...'

Kuat thought: 'Who do they think they're fooling? In all the years I've been governor of Xanadu this is the first time a Lord has been here. War hero of the battle of Styron IV indeed! Why, that's been over substantive months ago... He's had plenty of time to recover if it's really true he was wounded. No there's something more... they know or suspect something ... Well, we'll keep him busy. Shouldn't be hard to do here with all the pleasures Xanadu has to offer ... and there's Madu. No, he can't complain or he'll blow his cover ...'

And all the while, as the ornithopter neared, their destiny was approaching. He did not know that he was to be their destiny; he did not intend to be their destiny, and their destiny had not been predetermined.

The passenger in the descending ornithopter reached out with his mind to try to perceive the place, to sense it. It was hard, terribly hard ... there seemed to be a thick cloud-like cover – a mist – between his mind and the minds he tried to feel. Was it himself, his mind damage from the war? Or was it something more, the atmosphere of the planet – something to deter or prevent telepathy?

Lord bin Permaiswari shook his head. He was so full of self-doubt, so confused. Ever since the battle ... the mind-scarring probes of the fear machines ... how much permanent damage had they done? Perhaps here on Xanadu he could rest and forget.

As he stepped from the ornithopter Lord bin Permaiswari felt an even greater sense of bewilderment. He had known that Xanadu had no sun, but he was unprepared for the soft shadowless light which greeted him. The twin moons hung, seemingly, side by side, while their light was reflected by millions of mirrors. In the near distance li after li of white sand beaches stretched, while farther on stood chalk cliffs with the jet-black sea foaming at their bases. Black, white, silver, the colours of Xanadu.

Kuat approached him without delay. Kuat's sense of apprehension had diminished appreciably at the first glimpse of the Space Lord. The visitor did indeed look ill and confused: correspondingly, Kuat's amiability increased without conscious effort on his part.

'Xanadu extends you welcome, oh Lord bin Permaiswari. Xanadu and all that Xanadu contains is yours.' The traditional greeting sounded strange in his rough tones. The Space Lord saw before him a huge man, tall and correspondingly heavy, muscles gleaming, his longish reddish hair and beard showing magenta in the light of the moons and mirrors.

'It gives me pleasure, Governor Kuat, merely to be in Xanadu, and I return the planet and its contents to you,' replied Lord Kemal bin Permaiswari.

Kuat turned and gestured towards his two companions. 'This is Madu, a distant relative, and so my ward. And this is Lari, my brother, son of my father's fourth wife – she who drowned herself in the Sunless Sea.' The Space Lord winced at Kuat's laugh, but the young people appeared not to notice it.

Gentle Madu hid her disappointment and greeted the Lord with becoming modesty. She had expected (hoped for?) a shining figure, a blazing armour, or perhaps simply an aura which proclaimed 'I am a hero'. Instead she saw an intellectual-looking man, tired, looking somehow older than his substantive thirty years. She wondered what he had done, how this man could be the talk of the Instrumentality as the saviour of human culture in the battle of Styron IV.

Lari, because he was a male, knew more of the facts of the battle than Madu, and he greeted Lord bin Permaiswari with grave respect. In his dream world, second only to dancers and runners of easy grace, Lari looked up to intelligence. This was the man who had dared to pit himself, his living mind, his intellect against the dread fear machines ... and won! The price was evident in his face, but he had WON. Lari placed his hands together and held them to his forehead in a gesture of homage.

The Lord reached out in a gesture which won Lari's heart

forever. He touched Lari's hand and said, 'My friends call me Kemal'. Then he turned to include Madu and, almost as an afterthought, Kuat.

Kuat did not notice the near omission. He had turned and was walking towards what appeared to be a huge lump of yellow and black-striped fur. He made a peculiar hissing sound, and at once the lump separated into four enormous cats. Each cat was saddled, and each saddle was equipped with a holding ring, but there was no apparent means of guiding the cats.

Kuat answered Kemal's question. 'No, of course there's no way to guide them. They're pure cat, you know, unmodified except for size. No underpeople here! I think we're the only planet in the Instrumentality that doesn't have underpeople – except for Norstrilia, of course. But the reasons for Norstrilia and Xanadu are at the opposite ends of the spectrum. We enjoy our *senses* ... none of that nonsense about hard work building character like the Norstrilians believe. We don't believe in austerity and all that malarky. We just get more sensual pleasure out of our unmodified animals. We have robots to do the dirty work.'

Kemal nodded. After all, wasn't that what he was here for? To allow his senses to repair his damaged mind?

Nonetheless, the man who had faced the fear machines with scarcely a tremble did not know how to approach the cat which was designated as his.

Madu saw his hesitation. 'Griselda is perfectly friendly,' she said. 'Just wait a minute till I scratch her ears; then she'll lie down and you can mount.'

Kemal glanced up and caught an expression of disgust in Kuat's eyes. It did not help in his search for self-mending.

Madu, oblivious to Kuat's displeasure, had coaxed the great cat to kneeling position and smiled up at Kemal.

Kemal felt something like pain stab him at her glance. She

was so beautiful and so innocent; her vulnerability wrenched at his heart. He remembered the Lady Ru's quotation of an ancient sage: 'Innocence within is armour without', but a web of fear settled on his mind. He brushed it aside and mounted the cat.

As he lay dying nearly three centuries later, he remembered that ride. It was as thrilling as his first space jump. The leap into nothingness and then the sudden realization that he was travelling, travelling, travelling without volition, with no personal control over the direction his body might take. Before fear had the opportunity to assert itself it was converted into a visceral, almost orgasmic excitement, a gush of pleasure almost too strong to bear.

Lank dark hair flying in his face, the Lord bin Permaiswari would have been unrecognizable to the Lords and Ladies who gathered at the Bell on old Earth in time of crisis. They would not have recognized the boyish glee in a face which they were accustomed to seeing as grave and preoccupied. He laughed in the wind and tightened his knees against Griselda's flanks, holding the saddle ring with one hand as he turned back to wave at the others who were somewhat behind.

Griselda seemed to sense his pleasure at her long effortless bounds. Suddenly the ride took on a new proportion. Overhead the ornithopter which had brought the Space Lord to Xanadu passed by on its way back to the spaceport. At once Griselda left the pride and leapt futilely after the ascending ornithopter. As she attempted to bat at it, Kemal was forced to use both hands on the holding ring in order not to fall off ignominiously. She continued to leap and bat hopelessly in its direction until it disappeared from sight. Then she sat down to lick herself and, inadvertently, her passenger.

Lord Kemal found her sandpaper tongue not unpleasant,

but he winced as her fang brushed his leg. At some distance Kuat sat laughing. Madu's face, even in the distance showed concern, however, which cleared as the Lord waved to her. Lari, confident in the powers of the hero of Styron IV, was gazing dreamily at the distant city.

Slowly now, Griselda joined the rest of the pride, her attitude apparently one of some embarrassment at having performed such a kittenish prank when she had been entrusted with the welfare of the distinguished visitor.

In the distance the domes and towers of the city gleamed nacreous in the soft shadowless light of the moons and mirrors. Lord Kemal had his sense of unreality reinforced. The city looked so beautiful and so unreal that he had the feeling it might vanish as they approached. He was to learn that the city and all it stood for were all too real.

As they neared the city walls, Kemal could see that the stark whiteness of the city from afar was an illusion. The shimmering white walls of the buildings were set with gemstones in intricate patterns, flowers, leaves, and geometric designs all heightening the beauty of the incredible architecture. In all the worlds he had visited Lord Kemal had seen nothing to equal this city; Philip's palace on the Gem Planet was a hovel compared to these buildings.

Formal gardens with fountains and artificial pools separated the buildings. Shrubbery in an artful plan which gave the appearance of being natural was planted here and there. Suddenly the Space Lord realized another strange aspect of the planet: he had seen no trees.

Dogs yipped at them from safe distances as they entered the city, but this time Griselda refused to be tempted. Now that she was in the city she had assumed a certain dignity; it was as if she wanted to forget her previous dereliction. She headed straight for the palace steps.

Lord Kemal could feel the muscles of Griselda's haunches

tighten as she prepared to hurdle up the steps and through the open door. It would be a tight squeeze for the two of them. Fortunately Kuat reached the steps first and hissed his command to her. Kemal could feel her reluctance. She would much have preferred bounding up the steps, but she obeyed. She lay belly down, back feet crouched, front feet stretched forward; the Lord Kemal dismounted easily but with reluctance, a regret almost as great as Griselda's that the ride was over. He reached over to scratch the cat's ears.

Madu smiled approvingly. 'That's right. When you make friends with your cat, she'll obey you much more readily.'

Kuat grunted. 'I have my own way of making them obey if they get too many ideas of their own.' For the first time the Space Lord noticed a small barbed whip tucked into Kuat's belt, to which Kuat pointed now.

'Kuat, you wouldn't,' Madu protested. 'You never have . . .'

'You haven't seen me,' he said. Then as her face clouded he added as if reassuringly: 'Up to now I haven't needed to. But don't think I wouldn't.'

Kemal noticed that Kuat's reassurance was not quite adequate. A gauze of doubt or wonder seemed to obscure the open brightness of Madu's face. Once more the Lord Kemal felt a stab of fear for her and once more dismissed it.

It was her innocence he feared for. He found that her eyes reminded him of D'irena from the ancient days of his true youth – before he had been made wise in the ways of mankind, before he had been made to know that underpersons and true men could not mix as equals. D'irena with the fawnlike grace, the soft gentle mouth, the innocent eyes of the doe she was derived from. What had happened to her after he left? Did her eyes still hold that candid ingenuousness which he saw mirrored in Madu's eyes? Or had she mated with some gross stag and had some of his grossness transferred itself to her?

He hoped, remembering her fondly, that she had mated with a fine buck who had given her does as gentle and as graceful as she was in his memory. He shook his head. The fear machines had stirred up all kinds of strange memories and feelings. Absently, he petted the cat.

Servants came forward to unsaddle the cats. With a renewed start the Space Lord realized that these were true men, not underpersons, doing work, and he remembered Kuat's statement about enjoying the sensuality of animals. There was something else, something he had almost thought of, but he could not quite think ... it was as if he tried to catch the tail of an elusive animal as it disappeared around the corner.

Led by Kuat and trailed by Madu and Lari, the Lord Kemal threaded his way through a maze of rooms and corridors. Each seemed more amazing than the last. The only time the Space Lord had seen anything similar had been on the videotapes – a reconstruction of old Manhome as it had been before Radiation III. The walls were hung with tapestries and paintings based on reproductions of those from Earth; couches, statues, rugs of colour and warmth brought here by Xanadu's founder, the original Kahn. Yes, Xanadu was a return to pleasure of the senses, to luxury and beauty, to the unnecessary.

Kemal felt himself beginning to relax in this atmosphere of enchantment but the spell was broken when, upon reaching the main salon, Kuat unceremoniously flung himself into the nearest couch. As he stretched full length, he vaguely waved a hand to the rest of the party.

'Sit down, sit down,' he said. Candles flickered and glowed; low tables and couches stood about invitingly.

For the first time since the introduction on the Space Lord's arrival Lari spoke spontaneously. 'We welcome you to our home,' he said, 'and hope that we can do all possible to make your visit enjoyable'.

Kemal realized that he had paid little attention to the youth because he had been so absorbed in new impressions, and (he had to admit it to himself) the girl Madu had fascinated him. Lari, in his own way, was physically perfect as Madu. Tall, slender, lightly muscled, a golden boy. And, like Madu, he had a curious air of openness, of vulnerability. It seemed strange to the Lord Kemal that these two should grow up so innocent under the guardianship of a man as coarse and boorish as Kuat seemed.

Kuat interrupted his reverie. 'Come! The dju-di!'

Madu immediately moved towards a table on which rested a copper-coloured tray with silvery highlights. On the tray sat a dual-spouted pitcher of the same material and eight small matching goblets. A lid covered the top of the pitcher. As Madu picked up the pitcher, Kuat gave one of the grunts which the Space Lord was finding increasingly distasteful.

'Just be sure you put your thumb over the right hole.'

Her answering tone was indulgent but as nearly scornful as Kemal could imagine her being. 'I've been doing this since childhood. Is it likely I'd forget now?'

In after years it seemed to Kemal bin Permaiswari that this night was one of the important turns that his life took in its convoluted passage through time. He seemed removed from events as they occurred; he seemed a spectator, watching the actions, not only of the others but of himself as if he had no control over them, as if in a dream . . .

Madu knelt gracefully and placed a thumb over one of the two holes at the top of the pitcher. Candlelight played over the light silvery dusting of powder which covered the entire area of her bare skin. As she poured the reddish liquid into four of the little goblets, Kemal noticed that even the nails of her small hands were painted silver.

Kuat raised his goblet. The first toast by the rules of politeness should have been to the guest of honour, or at the very least to the Instrumentality, but Kuat went by his own rules.

'To pleasure,' he said, and drank the contents with one gulp.

While the rest of the party slowly sipped their drinks, Kuat roused himself to pour another cupful. He had swallowed the second cupful before the others had finished their first.

The Lord Kemal savoured the taste of the dju-di. Unlike anything he had ever tasted before, neither sweet nor sour. It was more like the juice of pomegranate than any other flavour he had tasted, and yet it was unique.

As he sipped he felt a pleasant tingling sensation pervade his body. By the time he had finished the cup he had decided that dju-di was the most delicious thing he had ever tasted. Instead of muddling his wits like alcohol or conferring nothing but sensual pleasure like the electrode, dju-di seemed to heighten all his senses, his awareness. All colours were brighter, background music of which he had been only dimly aware was suddenly piercingly lovely, the texture of the brocaded couch was a thing of joy, perfumes of flowers he had never known overwhelmed him. His scarred mind rejected Styron IV and all its implications. He felt a glow of comradeship, momentarily even towards Kuat, and suddenly felt he had come against a Diamoni wall.

Then he knew. His inability to sense or to read the other minds on the planet did not lie within himself or any defect incurred through the fear machines but was directly connected to Kuat, to some non-authorized barrier which Kuat had erected. The barrier was imperfect, however. Kuat had not been able merely to keep his own thoughts from being read; he had had to set up a universal barrier. This was obvious from the fact that Kuat showed no indication that he could sense the Space Lord.

'And what,' thought Kemal, 'do you have to hide? What is so much against the laws of the Instrumentality that you have had to set up a universal mind barrier?'

Kuat, relaxed, smiled pleasantly.

For the first time since Styron IV the Lord Kemal bin Permaiswari felt that he might in truth recover completely. It was the first time he had felt really interested in anything.

Madu brought him back to his present situation.

'You like our dju-di?' It was hardly a question.

Kemal nodded, blissful and still absorbed in the puzzle he had encountered.

'You may have one more,' she said, 'but that is all that is good for you. After that, one begins to lose one's senses, and *that*, after all, is *not* pleasurable, is it?'

She poured the second cup for Kemal, for Lari and herself.

Kuat reached for the pitcher, and she slapped playfully at his hand. 'One more and you might pour yourself pisang by accident.'

He laughed. 'I am bigger than most men and can drink more than they.'

'At least let me pour it then,' she said, and proceeded to do so.

She turned again to the Space Lord with a playful gaiety which did not ring quite true. 'He is one whom we must all indulge; but, really, it is dangerous to have too much. You see how this pitcher is made?'

She took off the lid to demonstrate the division of the pitcher. 'In one half is dju-di, in the other there is pisang which is identical in taste to dju-di, but it is deadly. One cup kills anyone drinking it within eefunjung.' Involuntarily Kemal shuddered. The unit of time she mentioned was so small as to be almost instantaneous.

'No antidote?'

'None.'

Lari, who had been sitting quietly, now spoke. 'It is the same thing, really. Dju-di is the distilled pisang. They come from a fruit which grows here, only on Xanadu. Galaxy knows how many people must have died eating the fruit or drinking the fermented but undistilled pisang before the secret of dju-di was discovered.'

'Worth every one of them,' Kuat laughed. Any remaining warmth engendered by the dju-di which the Space Lord might have felt towards Governor of Xanadu was dissipated, His curiosity regarding the duality of the pitcher, however, was aroused.

'But if you know that pisang is poison, why do you keep it in the same container with dju-di? For that matter why do you keep it in its undistilled state at all?'

Madu nodded agreement. 'I have often asked the same question, and the answers I get make no sense.'

'It's the excitement of danger,' Lari said. 'Don't you enjoy the dju-di more knowing there's the element of chance you'll get pisang?'

'That's what I said,' Madu repeated, 'the answers make no sense.'

At this point Kuat broke in. His speech was slightly slurred, but he spoke intelligently enough. 'In the first place, there is tradition. In the old days, under the first Khan and before Xanadu came under the jurisdiction of the Lords of the Instrumentality, there was a great deal of lawlessness on Xanadu. There were power struggles for leadership. People came here from other planets to plunder our richness. There had to be some simple way of eliminating them before they knew they were being eliminated. The double pitcher is copied, so they say, from a Chinesian one brought by the first Kahn. I don't know about that, but it has become traditional here. You won't find a dju-di holder on Xanadu without its corresponding pisang holder.' He nodded wisely as if he had explained everything, but the Space Lord was not satisfied.

'All right,' he said, 'you make the pitchers in the traditional way, but why, by Venus' cloud, must you continue to put pisang in them?'

Kuat's answer, when it came, was in even more slurred tones than his previous speech; the effects of too much dju-di began to make him sound intoxicated, and the Space Lord made mental note to heed Madu's injunctions not to exceed two cupfuls of the drink. Kuat gave a rather leering smile and wagged a finger admonishingly at Lord Kemal.

'Strangers mustn't ask too many questions. Might still be enemies around and we're all prepared. Anyway, that's the way we execute criminals on Xanadu.' His laugh was uninhibited. 'They don't know what they're getting. It's like a lottery. Sometimes I tease them a little. Give them dju-di first, and they start to think they're going to be freed. Then I give them another cup, and they don't suspect a thing. Drink it happily because nothing happened with the first cup. Then when the paralysis hits them – ha! you should see their faces!'

For an instant the latent dislike which the Space Lord had conceived for Kuat sprang full grown. But the man's intoxicated, in effect, he thought. And then: But is this the real man speaking?

'No, no, Kuat, you don't mean that!'

Realization seemed to return to Kuat. He gave his brother's knee a reassuring pat. 'No, no, course don't. Think I'll go to bed. You'll take care of guest, won't you?'

He staggered slightly as he stood up but managed to walk fairly steadily from the room.

Suddenly the barrier was down slightly. He could not read

Kuat's mind, but the Space Lord could sense, somewhere on the planet, something evil, strange, unlawful. A coldness seemed to replace the warmth of the dju-di in his veins.

Across the white dunes the wind was beginning to rise. Far from the city, protected by the ancient crater lake of the sunless sea, the laboratory had a deceptive exterior placidity. Within, the illegal diehr-dead, not yet quite sentient, stirred in their ambiotic fluid; outside, trees bearing their deadly fruit seemed to quiver as if in dread anticipation.

Madu sighed. 'I knew he shouldn't have had that last one, but he would do it.' She turned towards Lari, oblivious of the Space Lord, and said reassuringly.

'Of course he didn't mean what he said about teasing the prisoners. He's been so good to us all these years ... nobody could be so kind to us and cruel in other ways could he?'

Once more the Space Lord glanced in Lari's direction. The handsome young face, vital but young, so young, held a look of uneasiness. 'No, I suppose not, and still I've heard tales ...' He broke off remembering the presence of the Space Lord. 'Of course it's all nonsense,' he concluded, but Lord Kemal had the feeling that he was trying as much to reassure himself as to erase the bad impression his brother had made.

'We will eat now,' Madu said brightly, and stood up to go into the dining salon. Again the Space Lord felt as if the subject were being changed.

II

In after years the Space Lord remembered. Thoughts raced through his mind. *Oh, Xanadu, there is nothing with which to liken you in all the galaxies. The shadowless days and nights, the treeless plains, the sudden rainless blasts of thun-*

der and lightning which somehow add to your charm. Griselda. The only pure animal I ever knew. The great rumbling purr, the soft pink nose with the black spot on one side, the eyes which seemed to look beyond the features of my face into my very being. Oh Griselda, I hope that somewhere you still bound and leap . . .

But now: the first few days of the Lord Kemal bin Permaiswari on Xanadu passed quickly as he was introduced to the infinite pleasures of Xanadu.

On the day following Kemal's arrival a foot-race had been scheduled in which Lari was to run. The element of competition which had been brought back to Xanadu was part of a deliberate return to the simpler joys which mankind in its mechanization had forgotten.

Crowds at the stadium were gay and bright. Most of the young girls wore their hair loose and flowing; the women old and young alike, wore the typical costume of Xanadu: tiny short skirt and open sleeveless jacket. On most worlds the older women would have looked grotesque or at least ludicrous in this costume, and the younger women would have seemed lewd. But on Xanadu there was a basic innocence and acceptance of the body, and almost without exception the women of Xanadu, irrespective of age, seemed to have retained their lovely lithe figures, and there was no false modesty to call attention to their semi-nudity.

Most of the young people, male and female alike, wore the shimmering body powder which the Space Lord had first noted on Madu; some matched the powder to their clothes, others to their hair or eyes. A few wore a colourless luminescent dusting. Of them all, the Space Lord thought Madu the loveliest.

She radiated excitement, a portion of which communicated itself to Lord Kemal. Kuat seemed unemotional.

'How can you sit there so calmly?' she asked.

'The boy'll win, you know. Anyway horse racing is more exciting.'

'For you maybe. But not for me.'

Lord Kemal was interested. 'I have never seen this racing,' he said. 'What is it? The horses all run together to see which is the fastest?'

Madu nodded agreement. 'They all start at a given signal and run a predetermined path. The one who reaches the goal first is the winner. He,' she nodded her head playfully in Kuat's direction, 'likes to bet, that is to wager, that his horse will win. That is why he likes horse races better than human races.'

'And you have no wager on the human races?'

'Oh, no. It would be degrading to human beings to wager on their abilities or accomplishments!'

There were three races that day, each one narrowing the field of contestants. It became evident even in the first race that there was no real competition; Lari so far out-distanced the others that it was almost embarrassing. If he had not so obviously been a superb runner, it would have been easy to assume that the others had held back in order to allow the brother of the governor of Xanadu to win.

Kuat went off to the centre of the stadium to participate in a copy of an ancient ritual from old Manhome in which a crown of golden leaves was set on Lari's hair.

In his absence, Lord Kemal heard various whisperings behind him in which he caught the words 'dance with the aroi,' 'old governor will be pleased,' 'too bad his mother . . .' Madu seemed not to be listening.

After the celebrations when the Governor and his party had returned to the palace, Lord Kemal remembered the curious phrases; in particular he was puzzled by the present or future tense of 'old governor *will be* (not "would have been") pleased.' It stuck in his mind and fretted there, like a splinter in a sore finger. His mind was only just recovering from the wounds of the fear machines, and he decided he could not risk a further infection.

While Kuat was having his second goblet of dju-di, Lord Kemal said, most casually. 'How long have you been governor of Xanadu, Kuat?'

The latter glanced up, sensing something beneath the casualness of the immediate question.

Lari interrupted. 'I was a small baby –'

Kuat's gesture silenced him. 'For many years,' he said. 'Does it matter how many?'

'No, I was curious,' said the Space Lord, deciding on modified candour. 'I thought that the governorship of Xanadu was hereditary, but I heard something today which made me believe that the governor your father was still alive.'

Again Lari, before Kuat could silence him, rushed to answer. 'But he is. He's with the aroi . . . that's why my mother –'

Kuat's frown silenced him.

'These are not matters for the Instrumentality. These are matters of Xanadu's local customs, protected by Article No. 376984, sub-article *a*, paragraph 34c of the instrument under which Xanadu agreed to come under the protection of the Instrumentality. I can assure the Lord that only domestic matters of purely autochthonous origin are concerned.'

Lord Kemal nodded in ostensible agreement. He felt that he had somehow uncovered another small portion of the mystery which intrigued him, interested him as nothing else had done since Styron IV.

III

On the fourth 'day' of his stay on Xanadu, Lord Kemal went out with Madu and Lari for his first expedition beyond the walls of the city since his arrival. By this time, the Space Lord had become quite fond of the cat Griselda. It pleased him inordinately when she gave a great purr of pleasure and lay down for him to mount without awaiting a command.

He saw animals in a new light. With poignancy he knew that underpersons, modified animals in the shape of human beings were truly neither one thing nor the other. Oh, there were underpersons of great intelligence and power but . . . he let the thought trail off.

They raced across the plains with a singular joy. Windswept, treeless, the small planet had a wild beauty of its own. The black sea lashed at the foot of the chalk cliffs. Kemal, watching the li's of sand, felt the strangeness of the place once more. In the distance he saw a great bird rise, falter, then fall.

Later, much later, the song the computer wrote when he fed it the facts of time and place became known throughout the galaxies:

On a dark mountain
Alone in the cloud
The eagle paused
And the wind shrieked aloud
The thunder rolled

And the mist of the cloud
Formed the eagle's shroud
As it fell to the ground
Wings battered and torn.

And the surf
At the foot
Of the cliff
Was white
That night,
And bright
The wings
Of the falling
Bird.

I heard
The cry.

Perhaps it was a testimony to the depth of his feelings that the Lord Kemal fed these facts to the computer in such a way that some of his agony was expressed.

Madu and Lari watched also as the bird fell, their bright joy overcast by something they could not quite comprehend.

'But why?' Madu whispered. 'It flew along so freely as we were riding, we bounded as it soared all free and happy. And now ...'

'And now we must forget it,' said the Space Lord, of a wisdom born of endless endurance and a wariness he wished he did not feel. But he himself could not forget it. Hence the computer.

'On a dark mountain ...'

More slowly now, chilled by the death of beauty, of life, they proceeded, each involved in thought.

'What waste!' the Space Lord thought. What waste of beauty. The bird has soared free as a dream. Why? A strange current of air? Or something more deadly?

'What did my mother feel?' thought Lari. 'What were her feelings and thoughts when she walked into the warm deep dark sea – and knew she would never return?'

Madu felt confused and lonely. It was the first time that

she personally had ever confronted death in any form. Her parents were unreal to her; she had never known them. But this bird – she had seen it alive and free, flying, concerned with nothing more important than its graceful glides and soaring; and now, suddenly, it was dead. She could not reconcile the two thoughts in her mind.

It was Lord Kemal who, because of his age and experience, recovered first. 'You haven't told me,' he said, 'where we are going.'

Madu's smile was a feeble echo of her usual glow, but she made the effort. 'We're going to ride around the edge of the crater up there by the peak. It's a beautiful view, and when you stand there you can almost get the idea that you can see the whole planet.'

Lari nodded, determined to participate in the conversation despite the dark thoughts which had clouded his mind. 'It's true,' he said. 'You can even see the grove of buah trees from there. It's from the fruit of the buah tree that we get pisang and dju-di.'

'I was curious about that,' the Space Lord said. 'I haven't seen a tree since I landed on the planet.'

'No,' said Madu and Lari simultaneously. It created a small diversion, and they both laughed spontaneously, acting more naturally than they had since the death of the bird. Unconsciously they communicated their more cheerful attitude to the cats, which now began to bound forward once more at increased speed.

The Space Lord's happiness at the upswing in spirits of his young companions was tempered with chagrin that the conversation, which had started to be interesting, could not continue while their steeds were proceeding at this breakneck speed.

As they continued uphill, however, the cats gradually began to slow. The change was imperceptible at first, but as the long climb continued, Lord Kemal could feel Griselda's increasing effort. He had begun to think that nothing could tire her, but the climb to the edge of the crater was considerably longer than it looked from below.

That the other cats were also feeling the strain was evident from their decreased pace.

The Space Lord reopened the conversation. 'You were going to tell me about the trees,' he said.

It was Lari who answered first. 'You are quite right about not having seen any trees,' he said. 'The only trees which grow on Xanadu except the buah trees are the Kelapa trees, and they grow down in the craters of the smaller volcanoes. You can see some of *them* too when we get to the crater rim. But the buah trees always grow in groves – there must be both male and female to bear fruit, and the fruit can only be approached at certain times. Otherwise, even to inhale the scent is deadly.'

Madu gravely concurred. 'We must always keep at a distance from the buah grove until Kuat has consulted with the aroi, and when he tells us the time is right, then everyone on Xanadu participates in the harvest. The aroi dance, and it is the best time of all . . .'

Lari shook his head, disapprovingly. 'Madu, there are things we don't talk about to outsiders.'

Her face suffused, eyes suddenly welling, she stammered, 'But a Lord of the Instrumentality . . .'

Both men realized her unhappiness, and each in his own way hastened to remedy it. The Space Lord said, 'I'm good at not remembering things I shouldn't.'

Lari smiled at her and put his right hand hard on her shoulder. 'It's all right. He understands, and you didn't mean any harm. We won't either of us say anything to Kuat.'

As he lay in his room after dinner, the Space Lord tried to reconstruct the afternoon. They had reached the rim of the crater and it had been as Madu said: one could feel as if the horizon were infinite. The Space Lord had felt an overwhelming sense of the magnitude of infinity, something he had never quite experienced to this degree before in all of his trips through space or time. And yet there had been a small nagging feeling that something was not quite right.

Part of the feeling was associated with the grove of buah trees. He was sure that he had glimpsed a building as the uncertain, sometimes gusting, sometimes gentle wind blew the buah branches. He had not mentioned his observation to the young people. It was probably something else autochthonous and therefore forbidden to discussion, or surely one of them would have mentioned it.

He searched his memory (yes, he felt, his mind was definitely recovering) for a person among the servants at the palace who might be willing to talk to a Lord of Instrumentality. Suddenly he remembered something of which he must have made subliminal note at the time without being consciously aware. One of the men in the cat stable. What was it now? He had drawn a fish in the cat sand and then, glancing at the face of the Space Lord, had casually brushed it over. Later he had caught the gleam of metal at the man's neck. Could it have been a cross of the God Nailed High? Was there a member of the Old Strong Religion here on Xanadu? If so, he had a subject for blackmail.

Or did he? The man had been trying to communicate to him. Now that he thought of it, he was sure. Well, at least he had a possible colleague. Now all he had to do was remember the man's name.

He gave his mind free association; the face came to him; the man's hand fumbling at the chain at his neck ... yes, certainly the cross, he could see it now ... why hadn't he noticed it before? ... but there it was, recorded on his mind ... and yes, the man's name: Mr-Stokely-from-Boston. The unlikely suspicion that there was after all, an underperson on Xanadu crossed his mind. Mr-Stokely-from-Boston did not look as if he were animal-derived, but the name indicated something odd in his background.

Lord Kemal bin Permaiswari felt he could not wait until 'morning' to try to further his acquaintance with Mr-Stokely-from-Boston. What excuse could he have to go down to the cat stables at this hour? The gates of Xanadu were closed for the next eight hours. Then he realized that he had been thinking as an ordinary being. He was a Lord of the Instrumentality. Why should he have to have an excuse for anything he chose to do? Kuat might be Governor of Xanadu, but in the schema of the Instrumentality he was a very small speck.

Nevertheless, the Space Lord felt it best to be circumspect in his movements. Kuat had demonstrated his ruthlessness, and certain of these 'autochthonous' practices seemed very peculiar. A Space Lord who 'accidently' drank pisang while of a disordered mind might be written off. And there was the well-being of Mr-Stokely-from-Boston to be considered.

Griselda. That was the answer. He had noticed that she was sneezing this afternoon . . . he had even mentioned it to Madu and Lari . . . and they had passed it off as dust or pollen. But it would serve as an excuse. He had become so obviously fond of Griselda as to be the subject of teasing of a mild sort on her behalf. Certainly no one would find his concern for her out of the ordinary.

The corridors seemed strangely deserted as he strode through on his way to the cat stable. He realized that he had not ventured from his living area after the final meal of the day since his arrival on Xanadu. Apparently everyone retired after this meal, servants and masters alike. He wondered if the stables would also be deserted.

It was his incredible good fortune to find Mr-Stokely-from-Boston alone. At least, at the time, he assumed that the meeting was fortuitous. Later he questioned the bird-man. Mr-Stokely-from-Boston had proved to be, as the Space Lord had wildly surmised, an underperson.

Mr-Stokely-from-Boston's smile was wise and kindly. 'You see, Governor Kuat has no suspicion at all that I am an underperson. And, of course, the universal mind barrier has no operative effect on me. It was a little difficult, but I see I did manage to get through to you. I was somewhat worried when my mind probe showed all the leftover scar tissue from Styron IV, but I've been using the latest methods to try healing your mind, and I'm sure we're succeeding very nicely.'

The Space Lord felt an odd momentary resentment that this animal-derived person had such an intimate acquaintance with his mind, but the anger was short-lived because he quickly equated the empathy he had built up with Griselda to the mental communication he was having with the bird-man.

Mr-Stokely-from-Boston smiled even more broadly. 'I was quite right about you, Lord bin Permaiswari. You are the ally we have been needing here on Xanadu. You look surprised?'

Lord bin Permaiswari nodded. 'The governor was so firm that there were no underpersons on Xanadu –'

'Getting through has not been without its difficulties,' Mr-Stokely-from-Boston acknowledged, but I am not alone. And we have other human families, of course, but none so powerful as a Space Lord up to now.'

Lord Kemal found that he did not resent the assumption that he was an ally. Again the bird-man read his thoughts and smiled at him. He had a curiously winning smile, assured but kindly. He looked trustworthy, and Lord Kemal felt himself ready to accept whatever the bird-man might say.

Their thoughts locked. 'Let me introduce myself properly,' spieked the bird-man. 'My real name is E'duard, and my progenitor was the great E-telekeli, of whom you may have heard.'

Lord Kemal found the false modesty of this statement rather touching. He bowed his head momentarily in respect; the legendary bird-man, the E-telekeli, was known throughout the Instrumentality as the acknowledged leader and spiritual adviser of the underpersons. This egg-derived underperson could be a most helpful ally in carrying out the work of the Instrumentality or an opposition of fearful proportions. The Lords and Ladies who ruled the Instrumentality were anxious for his co-operation.

Many underpersons were known to have extraordinary medical and psychic powers, and it comforted the Space Lord to know that the animal-derived person who had been manipulating his mind was a descendant of the E-telekeli. He found that he was spieking his thought because E'duard could obviously hier them. It would certainly make the process of solving Xanadu's system simpler for the Space Lord if they co-operated, but first he wanted to know if their peculiar alliance violated any of the laws of the Instrumentality.

'No,' E'duard was emphatic. 'In fact, it is a correction of matters which are in direct conflict with the laws of the Instrumentality, with which we have to deal.'

'Something "autochthonous"?' asked the Space Lord shrewdly.

'Native culture is involved,' E'duard agreed, 'but it's really being used as a screen for something far more evil – and I use the word "evil" not only in this sense' (he held up the cross of the God Nailed High) 'but in its sense of the basic violation of the rights of the living. I mean the right of an eternity to exist, to exist on its own terms provided they do not violate the rights of others, to come to its own terms with life, and to make its own decisions.'

For a second time Lord Kemal Permaiswari nodded in respect and agreement. 'These are inalienable rights.'

E'duard shook his head. 'They *should* be,' he spieked, 'but on Xanadu, Kuat has found a way around that inalienability. You are, of course, familiar with the diehr-dead?'

'Of course. "And ne'er a life of their own . . ." ' he quoted from an ancient song. 'But what does that have to do with the rights of the living? The diehr-dead are grown from the frozen bits of flesh of remarkable achievers long dead. It's true that in regenerating the physical person of the dead one we have sometimes had extraordinary results with the diehr-dead in their second lives; but sometimes not – their achievements seem to have been a combination of circumstances and genes, not of genes alone . . .'

Again E'duard shook his head. 'It's not of the legal, scientifically controlled diehr-dead I spiek, although I sometimes feel very sorry for them. But what would you think of diehr-dead grown from the living?'

The Space Lord looked his wonder and horror as E'duard continued. 'Diehr-dead who are controlled like puppets by Kuat, diehr-dead who are substituted for the originals, so that in truth neither the diehr-deads nor the original has a life of its own . . .'

With quick realization the Space Lord knew what was in the building he had glimpsed in the grove of buah trees. 'That's the laboratory, isn't it?'

E'duard nodded. 'It's a perfect location. Kuat has spread the rumour that the scent of the buah tree is deadly except when, after consultation with the aroi, he pronounces it safe to harvest the fruit. So nobody dares approach the laboratory. All nonsense. There is only a very short period, just before harvest, when the scent of the buah fruit is deadly . . . in other words, just enough truth to the rumour to give it currency. You saw our scout killed this morning –'

Lord Kemal looked uncomprehending. 'The unmodified eagle you saw fall from the skies this morning on your ride. He was scouting the laboratory for us. He was shot with a pisang dart. It's things like that which make people believe they must stay away from the grove.'

'You could communicate?'

For the first time the Space Lord thought that the smile of the bird-man was a little smug. 'Of course.' Then his face fell and his eyes became old and sad. 'He was a brother of mine; we were hatched in the same nest, but I was chosen for genetic coding as an underperson, and he was not. Our feelings are somewhat different from those of true persons, but we are capable of love and loyalty, and sadness as well . . .'

Lord Kemal saw again in memory the handsome soaring bird of his morning's ride, and felt E'duard's sadness. Yes he could believe in the feelings of the underpersons. E'duard touched his hand with a tentative finger.

'I could tell that you grieved for him without knowing any of the circumstances. It is one of the reasons I willed you to come tonight.' There was a quick change in his mood. 'We must deal first with the aroi.'

'I have heard the word, but I don't know its meaning,' the Space Lord acknowledged

'I'm not surprised. The aroi lead a life of pleasure; they sing, they dance, they entertain and they serve as a kind of priesthood. Both men and women make up the aroi, and they are respected and honoured. But there's a singularly ghastly requirement for joining the aroi.'

The Space Lord looked his question.

'All living descendants of the current mate of the person joining the aroi must be sacrificed. Or the mate must die, and if there is more than one offspring of that union, an equivalent number of other volunteers must also die.'

Lord Kemal comprehended. 'So that is the reason that Lari's mother drowned herself in the sunless sea – to save her infant son. But why did the old Governor join the aroi?'

'Don't you see? With Kuat as Governor and the old Governor with the aroi, that pair of conspirators wields a power over this planet so absolute –'

'So it was a conspiracy from the beginning.'

'Of course. Kuat was the son of the first wife, when the governor was in his first youth. In his old age he wanted to continue the power but with the help of a viceroy, as it were.'

'And the diehr-dead in the laboratory?'

'That is the reason that the matter is urgent. They are full-grown and almost sentient. They must be destroyed before they are substituted for the originals and the originals killed.'

'I suppose there is no other way, but it seems almost like murder.'

E'duard disagreed. 'The substitution is both physical and spiritual murder. These diehr-dead are like robots without soul –' He saw the Space Lord's faint smile. '– I know you do not believe in the Old Strong Religion, but I think you know what I mean.'

'Yes. They are not, in the sense you mean, living beings. They have no will of their own.'

'The aroi are two villages away, about 100 li. After they have performed their entertainment in those villages, they will proceed to here. That will be the signal for the harvest of the buah fruit and the substitution of the diehr-dead for their living counterparts. Then there will be no opposition to Kuat on the planet, and he can give his cruelty full rein ... and plan for the conquest of other worlds. His brother Lari is one of his planned victims because he fears the boy's popularity with the crowds.'

The Space Lord was almost incredulous. 'But the two persons he has seemed to be truly fond of are Lari and the girl Madu.'

'Nevertheless one of the diehr-dead in the laboratory is a replica of the boy, Lari.'

'Won't the old Governor, the father, object?'

'Possibly, although the mere fact that he joined the aroi when he knew what the cost would be in human terms argues against his interference.'

'And Madu?'

'He will keep her as she is, for the time being, and try to mould her to his will. He so little respects individuality that if he cannot, he will obtain some bit of her flesh and eventually she too will be replaced by a diehr-dead. He could be satisfied with a physical replica without caring that the *person* was missing.'

The Space Lord felt his tired mind attempting to ingest more than was possible at one time. Immediately E'duard was sympathetic.

'I have kept you too long. You must rest. We will be in touch. And don't worry, Kuat's mind barrier applies to him too; only underpersons and animals are exempt, and we are all in league.'

As he made his way back to his living quarters, Lord bin Permaiswari was again aware of the silence, the absence of any human activity anywhere in the palace. He wondered how long it had been since he had left his room to seek Mr-Stokely-from-Boston in the cat stables. He wished he had remembered to ask E'duard how he had acquired that unlikely name. Immediately he was aware of E'duard's voice spieking in his mind: 'It was bestowed upon me for some small service I rendered the Instrumentality on old Manhome.' The Space Lord started with surprise. He had forgotten that there were no space barriers to spieking if he left his mind open. He spieked 'Thank you,' then closed his mind.

VI

When he awoke from a dream-tormented sleep, the Space Lord felt a weariness which he knew E'duard would have termed a tiredness of the soul. There was no way in which he could communicate with the Instrumentality. The next scheduled spaceship for the spaceport above Xanadu was too far in the future to be of any use in the matter of the illegal diehr-dead. E'duard was right. The substitution must be stopped before it began. But how? He felt it somehow belittling to his position for a Space Lord to have to rely on an underperson; the only consolation was that the underperson involved was a descendant of the great E-telekeli.

As they ate their first meal of the day, Madu seemed subdued; Lari was not present. Lord Kemal, making his voice as pleasant as he could, queried Kuat about the boy.

'He's gone down to Raraku to dance with the aroi,' Kuat said. Then apparently, he realized that the Space Lord would not know the word 'aroi'. 'It's a group of dancers and entertainers we have here on Xanadu,' he explained kindly. Kemal felt a coldness about his heart.

He could hardly wait to communicate with E'duard. 'Lari is missing,' he spieked, as soon as he was sure that Kuat would not notice his expression.

'All the diehr-dead are still in place, our scouts report,' E'duard spieked back. 'We will try to locate him and communicate with you.'

But time passed; the only things the underpersons were able to assure Lord Kemal were that Lari was not with the aroi at Raraku and that the diehr-dead replica of him was still in place in the laboratory. He seemed to have vanished from the planet.

Madu had taken Kuat's statement at its face value; she was

much quieter now, but she apparently believed that Lari was dancing with the aroi. The Space Lord tried a gentle probing.

'I had gathered from what I heard that the aroi was a closed group which one had to join in order to participate.'

'Oh, yes, to participate fully,' Madu said, 'but near harvest time the best dancers are allowed to dance with the aroi whether they are members or not. It will not be so long now. The aroi have moved from Raraku to Poike. Then they will come here. I will be so glad to see Lari again; I always miss him when he goes off to run or dance.'

'He has gone away before to dance?' the Space Lord asked.

'Well, no. Not to dance. To run, but not to dance before. But he is very good. He really hasn't been quite old enough before.'

'And do you have other entertainments at the harvest besides the dancing?' the Space Lord asked, still seeking a clue as to the whereabouts of the vanished Lari.

Her smile had some of its old radiance. 'Oh, yes. That is when we have the horse racing I told you about. It is Kuat's favourite sport. Only,' her face clouded, 'this time I'm afraid his horse doesn't have much chance of winning. Gogle has really been raced too long and too hard; his back legs are wearing out. The vet was talking about doing a muscle transplant if they had a suitable donor, but I don't think they've found one.'

At the prospect of seeing Lari soon again, however, she seemed happier with some of the joy the Space Lord associated with her. They went for a cat ride, and Lord Kemal felt again the overwhelming sense of wonder and pleasure as he and the cat Griselda became as one being. Their feelings were in such close communication that he did not have to tighten his knees or hiss at her to obey his slightest wish. For the first time in days Lord bin Permaiswari was able to forget about E'duard and the diehr-dead, about his concern for Lari and his worry as to whether the Instrumentality would approve his co-operation with the bird-man.

For the first time, also, the Space Lord began to wonder to what extent Madu and Lari were committed to each other. Now that he had Madu to himself, he felt more than ever the strong attraction she held for him. He had never, in all the worlds he had known, felt such an attraction for a woman before. And, such was his honour, he began to feel it all the more imperative to restore Lari safely before he could express his feelings to her. He tried spieking to E'duard.

'Nothing,' said the bird-man. 'We have found no trace of him. The last time he was seen by one of our people was on the outskirts of the palace, headed in the direction of the stables. That is all.'

On the day of the festival before the harvest the Space Lord, using Griselda as a pretext, once more went to the cat stables.

E'duard as Mr-Stokely-from-Boston was hard at work. He looked gravely at the Space Lord, but his mind remained closed. He did not spiek. Lord bin Permaiswari found himself annoyed. He opened his mind and spieked 'Animals!'

E'duard winced slightly but still did not spiek.

The Space Lord, apologetic, spieked. 'I'm sorry. I didn't mean that.'

This time E'duard spieked back. 'Yes, you did. And we are, but why so much contempt? We are each what we are.'

'I was annoyed that your mind was closed to me, a Space Lord. You have the right to close your mind to anyone. I apologize.'

E'duard accepted the statement graciously. He said, 'There was a reason that my mind was closed to you. I was trying to decide how to tell you something. And I needed to know your full feelings about the girl Madu and the boy Lari before I can spiek freely.'

Lord bin Permaiswari felt a sense of shame; he had behaved, not as a Space Lord, but as a child. He tried to spiek with complete frankness. 'I am truly worried about the boy Lari. As to Madu, you must know that there is a strong attraction, but I must first find out about the boy and see what her feelings are.'

E'duard nodded. 'You spiek as I hoped you would. We have found Lari. He is crippled for life.'

Lord Kemal's intake of air hurt his throat. 'What do you mean?'

'Kuat had his vet take the boy's calf muscles and transplant them to his favourite horse, Gogle. The horse will be able to run one more race at top speed, thus fooling all of those who bet against Kuat. It's improbable that any surgery will enable the boy to walk again, much less to run or dance.'

The Space Lord found his mind a blank. He realized that E'duard was still spieking.

'We will have the boy in his wheelchair at the horse race tomorrow. You will need Madu's help. Then you can decide what to do.'

Until the time of the race next day Lord Kemal found himself moving as if in a dream, dispassionately observing his movements. E'duard spieked to him only once. 'We must kill off the diehr-dead at once,' he said. 'After the race tomorrow, when everybody is celebrating will be the time. Keep Kuat busy and I will take care of the matter.'

Fearful, unhappy, feeling weaker than he had since Styron IV, Lord Kemal bin Permaiswari accompanied Madu and Governor Kuat to the horse race. At their box sat Lari, white-faced, thin, much older, in a wheelchair. 'Why?' spiek-shrieked the Space Lord.

E'duard's voice came through much more calmly. 'Kuat actually thought he was being kind. With the boy crippled, he can't be the race-hero he has been to the people of Xanadu.

Kuat thought that that way he wouldn't need to substitute the diehr-dead. He didn't realize he's taken away the boy's chief reason for wanting to live; he might almost as well have substituted the diehr-dead.'

Madu was sobbing. Kuat, in what he intended as a rough kindness, stroked her hair. 'We'll take care of him. And, Venus! Will we fool the bettors today! They think Gogle can't run any more. Will they be fooled! Of course, it's only for this one race, but it'll be worth it!'

'Be worth it,' the Space Lord thought. Be worth the rest of Lari's life, spent crippled, unable to do what he loved most.

'Be worth it,' Madu thought. Never to dance again, never to run, to feel the wind in his hair as the crowds cheered.

'Be worth it,' Lari thought. What does anything matter any more.

Gogle won by half a track.

Kuat, his mood expansive, said to the others, 'See you in the main salon of the palace. Have to collect my wagers.'

Madu's face was carved of marble as she wheeled Lari towards a special two-cat cart brought up beside the stadium. Lord Kemal, without a word, mounted Griselda. He felt the need, for a little while, at least, for solitude.

They loped, in silent communication, away from the walls of the city. Lord Kemal heard a cry from the city gate, but he paid no attention. His mind was on Lari. Again the cry. Another lope. Suddenly Griselda faltered, stumbled, fell. At once the Space Lord was down, beside her face. Her eyes were glazing. He saw, then, the dart piercing her neck. Pisang. She tried to lick his hand; he petted her, his eyes filled with tears. She gave one great wretching sigh, looked into his being, shuddered and died. Part of him died with her.

When he reached the gate he queried the guard. No one was supposed to leave the city between the end of the races and the harvesting of the buah fruit. Griselda was the victim of an error of administrative oversight. No one had remembered to tell the Space Lord.

Silently he walked back through the pathways of the city. How beautiful it had seemed to him a short while ago. How empty and how sad it seemed now.

He reached the main salon shortly after Madu and Lari in his wheelchair arrived.

It was strange how all the budding desire for Madu had withered like a flower in the frost.

Kuat entered, laughing.

Lord Kemal would be tortured for more than two centuries by a question. When did the ends justify the means? When was the law absolute? He saw in his mind's eye Griselda bounding over dunes and plains – a Madu innocent as dawn – Lari dancing under a sunless moon.

'Dju-di !' demanded Kuat.

Madu moved gracefully towards the low table. She picked up the two-holed pitcher. Lord Kemal saw, through E'duard's spiech, that the pisang flow was being let into the ambiotic fluid of the diehr-dead. Soon they would be truly dead.

Kuat laughed. 'I won every bet I made today.'

He looked away from Madu towards the Lord Kemal.

Almost imperceptibly Madu's thumb moved from one hole to the other.

Lord Kemal did nothing in the endless night.

Retrograde Summer

John Varley

Science fiction is continually enriched by the advent of fine new writers, and 1975 saw the remarkable flowering of the talents of John Varley, whose first story had been published just a year before and who was a nominee for the John W. Campbell Award for new sf writers. This best-of-the-year book contains two of Varley's stories, an achievement equalled before only by Robert Silverberg. Varley is a remarkable writer, and if you feel a similarity in this story to the work of Robert A. Heinlein, don't be too surprised: Varley has been a Heinlein fan for many years, and this imaginative story of life on a Mercury colony rivals the best of Heinlein in fascination.

I was at the spaceport an hour early on the day my clone-sister was to arrive from Luna. Part of it was eagerness to see her. She was three E-years older than me, and we had never met. But I admit that I grab every chance I can get to go to the port and just watch the ships arrive and depart. I've never been off-planet. Someday I'll go, but not as a paying passenger. I was about to enrol in pilot-training school.

Keeping my mind on the arrival time of the shuttle from Luna was hard, because my real interest was in the liners departing for all the far-off places in the system. On that very day the *Elizabeth Browning* was lifting off on a direct, high-gee run for Pluto, with connections for the cometary zone.

She was sitting on the field a few kilometres from me, on-boarding passengers and freight. Very little of the latter. The *Browning* was a luxury-class ship, where you paid a premium fare to be sealed into a liquid-filled room, doped to the gills and fed through a tube for the five-gee express run. Nine days later, at wintertime Pluto, they decanted you and put you through ten hours of physical rehabilitation. You could have made it in fourteen days at two gees and only have been mildly uncomfortable, but maybe it's worth it to some people. I had noticed that the *Browning* was never crowded.

I might not have noticed the arrival of the Lunar shuttle, but the tug was lowering it between me and the *Browning*. They were berthing it in Bay 9, a recessed area a few hundred metres from where I was standing. So I ducked into the tunnel that would take me there.

I arrived in time to see the tug cut the line and shoot into space to meet the next incoming ship. The Lunar shuttle was a perfectly reflective sphere sitting in the middle of the landing bay. As I walked up to it, the force-field sprang into being over the bay, cutting off the summertime sunlight. The air started rushing in, and in a few minutes my suit turned off. I was suddenly sweating, cooking in the heat that hadn't been dissipated as yet. My suit had cut off too soon again. I would have to have that checked. Meantime, I did a little dance to keep my bare feet away from the too-hot concrete.

When the air temperature reached the standard 24 degrees, the field around the shuttle cut off. What was left behind was an insubstantial latticework of decks and bulkheads, with people gawking out of the missing outer walls of their rooms.

I joined the crowd of people clustered around the ramp. I had seen a picture of my sister, but it was an old one. I wondered if I'd recognize her.

There was no trouble. I spotted her at the head of the ramp, dressed in a silly-looking loonie frock coat and carrying a pressurized suitcase. I was sure it was her because she looked just like me, more or less, except that she was a female and she was frowning. She might have been a few centimetres taller than me, but that was from growing up in a lower gravity field.

I pushed my way over to her and took her case.

'Welcome to Mercury,' I said, in my friendliest manner. She looked me over. I don't know why, but she took an instant dislike to me, or so it seemed. Actually, she had disliked me before we ever met.

'You must be Timmy,' she said. I couldn't let her get away with that. There are limits.

'Timothy. And you're my sister, Jew.'

'Jubilant.'

We were off to a great start.

She looked around her at the bustle of people in the landing bay. Then she looked overhead at the flat-black underside of the force-roof and seemed to shrink away from it.

'Where can I rent a suit?' she asked. 'I'd like to get one installed before you have a blowout here.'

'It isn't that bad,' I said. 'We do have them more often here than you do in Luna, but it can't be helped.' I started off in the direction of the General Environments, and she fell in beside me. She was having difficulty walking. I'd hate to be a loonie; just about anywhere they go, they're too heavy.

'I was reading on the trip that you had a blowout here at the port only four lunations ago.'

I don't know why, but I felt defensive. I mean, sure we have blowouts here, but you can hardly *blame* us for them. Mercury has a lot of tidal stresses; that means a lot of quakes. Any system will break down if you shake it around enough.

'All right,' I said, trying to sound reasonable. 'It happens I was here during that one. It was in the middle of the last darkyear. We lost pressure in about ten per cent of the passages, but it was restored in a few minutes. No lives were lost.'

'A few minutes is more than enough to kill someone without a suit, isn't it?' How could I answer that? She seemed to think she had won a point. 'So I'll feel a lot better when I get into one of your suits.'

'Okay, let's get a suit into you.' I was trying to think of something to re-start the conversation and drawing a blank. Somehow she seemed to have a low opinion of our environmental engineers on Mercury and was willing to take her contempt out on me.

'What are you training for?' I ventured. 'You must be out of school. What are you going to do?'

'I'm going to be an environmental engineer.'

'Oh.'

I was relieved when they finally had her lie on the table, made the connection from the computer into the socket at the back of her head, and turned off her motor control and sensorium. The remainder of the trip to GE had been a steady lecture about the shortcomings of the municipal pressure service in Mercury Port. My head was swimming with facts about quintuple-redundant failless pressure sensors, self-sealing locks, and blowout drills. I'm *sure* we have all those things, and just as good as the ones in Luna. But the best anyone can do with the quakes shaking everything up a hundred times a day is achieve a ninety-nine per cent safety factor. Jubilant had sneered when I trotted out that figure. She quoted one to me with fifteen decimal places, all of them nines. That was the safety factor in Luna.

I was looking at the main reason why we didn't need that kind of safety, right in the surgeon's hands. He had her chest opened up and the left lung removed, and he was placing the suit generator into the cavity. It looked pretty much like the lung he had removed except that it was made of metal and had a mirror finish. He hooked it up to her trachea and the stump ends of the pulmonary arteries and did some adjustments. Then he closed her and applied somatic sealant to the incisions. In thirty minutes she would be ready to wake up, fully healed. The only sign of the operation would be the gold button of the intake valve under her left collarbone. And if the pressure were to drop by two millibars in the next instant, she would be surrounded by the force field that is a Mercury suit. She would be safer than she had ever been in her life, even in the oh-so-safe warrens in Luna.

The surgeon made the adjustment in my suit's brain while Jubilant was still out. Then he installed the secondary items in her; the pea-sized voder in her throat so she could talk without inhaling and exhaling, and the binaural radio receptors in her middle ears. Then he pulled the plug out of her brain, and she sat up. She seemed a little more friendly. An hour of sensory deprivation tends to make you more open and relaxed when you come out of it. She started to get back into her loonie coat.

'That'll just burn off when you go outside,' I pointed out.

'Oh, of course. I guess I expected to go by tunnel. But you don't have many tunnels here, do you?'

You can't keep them pressurized, can you?

I really *was* beginning to feel defensive about our engineering.

'The main trouble you'll have is adjusting to not breathing.'

We were at the west portal, looking through the force-curtain that separated us from the outside. There was a warm breeze drifting away from the curtain, as there always is in summer time. It was caused by the heating of the air next to the curtain by the wave-lengths of light that are allowed to pass through so we can see what's outside. It was the beginning of retrograde summer, when the sun backtracks at the zenith and gives us a triple helping of very intense light and radiation. Mercury Port is at one of the hot-spots, where retrograde sun motion coincides with solar noon. So even though the force-curtain filtered out all but a tiny window of visible light, what got through was high-powered stuff.

'Is there any special trick I should know?'

I'll give her credit; she wasn't any kind of fool; she was just over-critical. When it came to the operation of her suit, she was completely willing to concede that I was the expert.

'Not really. You'll feel an overpowering urge to take a breath after a few minutes, but it's all psychological. Your blood will be oxygenated. It's just that your brain won't feel right about it. But you'll get over it. And don't try to breath when you talk. Just sub-vocalize, and the radio in your throat will pick it up.'

I thought about it and decided to throw in something else, free of charge.

'If you're in the habit of talking to yourself, you'd better try to break yourself of it. Your voder will pick it up if you mutter, or sometimes if you just think too loud. Your throat moves sometimes when you do that, you know. It can get embarrassing.'

She grinned at me, the first time she had done it. I found myself liking her. I had always *wanted* to, but this was the first chance she had given me.

'Thanks. I'll bear it in mind. Shall we go?'

I stepped out first. You feel nothing at all when you step through a force-curtain. You can't step through it at all unless you have a suit generator installed, but with it turned on, the field just forms around your body as you step through. I turned around and could see nothing but a perfectly flat, perfectly reflective mirror. It bulged out as I watched in the shape of a nude woman, and the bulge separated from the curtain. What was left was a silver-plated Jubilant.

The suit generator causes the field to follow the outlines of your body, but from one to one and a half millimetres from the skin. It oscillates between those limits, and the changing volume means a bellows action forces the carbon dioxide out through your intake valve. You expel waste gas and cool yourself in one operation. The field is perfectly reflective except for two pupil-sized discontinuities that follow your eye movements and let in enough light to see by, but not enough to blind you.

'What happens if I open my mouth?' she mumbled. It takes a while to get the knack of sub-vocalizing clearly.

'Nothing. The field extends over your mouth, like it does over your nostrils. It won't go down your throat.'

A few minutes later: 'I sure would like to take a breath.' She would get over it. 'Why is it so hot?'

'Because at the most efficient setting your suit doesn't release enough carbon dioxide to cool you down below about thirty degrees. So you'll sweat a bit.'

'It feels like thirty-five or forty.'

'It must be your imagination. You can change the setting by turning the nozzle of your air valve, but that means your tank will be releasing some oxygen with the CO_2, and you never know when you'll need it.'

'How much of a reserve is there?'

'You're carrying forty-eight hours worth. Since the suit releases oxygen directly into your blood, we can use about ninety-five per cent of it, instead of throwing most of it away to cool you off, like your loonie suits do.' I couldn't resist that one.

'The term is Lunarian,' she said, icily. Oh, well. I hadn't even known the term was derogatory.

'I think I'll sacrifice some margin for comfort now. I feel

bad enough as it is in this gravity without stewing in my own sweat.'

'Suit yourself. You're the environment expert.'

She looked at me, but I don't think she was used to reading expressions on a reflective face. She turned the nozzle that stuck out above her left breast, and the flow of steam from it increased.

'That should bring you down to about twenty degrees, and leave you with about thirty hours of oxygen. That's under ideal conditions, of course; sitting down and keeping still. The more you exert yourself, the more oxygen the suit wastes keeping you cool.'

She put her hands on her lips. 'Timothy, are you telling me that I shouldn't cool off? I'll do whatever you say.'

'No, I think you'll be all right. It's a thirty-minute trip to my house. And what you say about the gravity has merit; you probably need the relief. But I'd turn it up to twenty-five as a reasonable compromise.'

She silently readjusted the valve.

Jubilant thought it was silly to have a traffic conveyor that operated in two-kilometre sections. She complained to me the first three or four times we got off the end of one and stepped on to another. She shut up about it when we came to a section knocked out by a quake. We had a short walk between sections of the temporary slideway, and she saw the crews working to bridge the twenty-metre gap that had opened beneath the old one.

We only had one quake on the way home. It didn't amount to anything; just enough motion that we had to do a little dance to keep our feet under us. Jubilant didn't seem to like it much. I wouldn't have noticed it at all, except Jubilant yelped when it hit.

*

Our house at that time was situated at the top of a hill. We had carried it up there after the big quake seven darkyears before that had shaken down the cliffside where we used to live. I had been buried for ten hours in that one – the first time I ever needed digging out. Mercurians don't like living in valleys. They have a tendency to fill up with debris during the big quakes. If you live at the top of a rise, you have a better chance of being near the top of the rubble when it slides down. Besides, my mother and I both liked the view.

Jubilant liked it, too. She made her first comment on the scenery as we stood outside the house and looked out over the valley we had just crossed. Mercury Port was sitting atop the ridge, thirty kilometres away. At that distance you could just make out the hemispherical shape of the largest buildings.

But Jubilant was more interested in the mountains behind us. She pointed to a glowing violet cloud that rose from behind one of the foothills and asked me what it was.

'That's quicksilver grotto. It always looks like that at the start of retrograde summer. I'll take you over there later. I think you'll like it.'

Dorothy greeted us as we stepped through the wall.

I couldn't put my finger on what was bothering mom. She seemed happy enough to see Jubilant after seventeen years. She kept saying inane things about how she had grown and how pretty she looked. She had us stand side by side and pointed out how much we looked like each other. It was true, of course, since we were genetically identical. She was five centimetres taller than me, but she could lose that in a few months in Mercury's gravity.

'She looks just like you did two years ago, before your last Change,' she told me. That was a slight misstatement; I hadn't been quite as sexually mature the last time I was a female. But she was right in essence. Both Jubilant and I were genotypically male, but mom had had my sex changed when I first came to Mercury, when I was a few months old. I had spent the first fifteen years of my life female. I was thinking of Changing back, but wasn't in a hurry.

'You're looking well yourself, Glitter,' Jubilant said.

Mom frowned for an instant. 'It's Dorothy now, honey. I changed my name when we moved here. We use Old Earth names on Mercury.'

'I'm sorry, I forgot. My mother always used to call you Glitter when she spoke of you. Before she, I mean before I...'

There was an awkward silence. I felt like something was being concealed from me, and my ears perked up. I had high hopes of learning some things from Jubilant, things that Dorothy had never told me no matter how hard I prodded her. At least I knew where to start in drawing Jubilant out.

It was a frustrating fact at that time that I knew little of the mystery surrounding how I came to grow up on Mercury instead of in Luna, and why I had a clone-sister. Having a clone twin is a rare enough thing that it was inevitable I'd try to find out how it came to pass. It wasn't socially debilitating, like having a fraternal sibling or something scandalous like that. But I learned early not to mention it to my friends. They wanted to know how it happened, how my mom managed to get around the laws that forbid that kind of unfair preference. One Person, One Child; that's the first moral lesson any child learns, even before Thou Shalt Not Take a Life. Mom wasn't in jail, so it must have been legal. But how? And why? She wouldn't talk, but maybe Jubilant would.

Dinner was eaten in a strained silence, interrupted by awkward attempts at conversation. Jubilant was suffering from culture shock and an attack of nerves. I could understand it, looking around me with her eyes. Loonies, pardon me, Lunarians, live all their lives in burrows down in the rock and come to need the presence of solid substantial walls around them. They don't go outside much. When they do, they are wrapped in a steel and plastic cocoon that they can feel around them, and they look out of it through a window. She was feeling terribly exposed and trying to be brave about it. When inside a force-bubble house, you might as well be sitting on a flat platform under the blazing sun. The bubble is invisible from the inside.

When I realized what was bothering her, I turned up the polarization. Now the bubble looked like tinted glass.

'Oh, you needn't,' she said, gamely. 'I have to get used to it. I just wish you had *walls* somewhere I could look at.'

It was more apparent than ever that something was upsetting Dorothy. She hadn't noticed Jubilant's unease, and that's not like her. She should have had some curtains rigged to give our guest a sense of enclosure.

I did learn some things from the intermittent conversation at the table. Jubilant had divorced her mother when she was ten E-years old, an absolutely extraordinary age. The only grounds for divorce at that age are really incredible things like insanity or religious evangelism. I didn't know much about Jubilant's foster mother – not even her name – but I did know that she and Dorothy had been good friends back in Luna. Somehow, the question of how and why Dorothy had abandoned her child and taken me, a chip off the block, to Mercury, was tied up in that relationship.

'We could never get close, as far back as I can remember,' Jubilant was saying. 'She told me crazy things, she didn't seem to fit in. I can't really explain it, but the court agreed with me. It helped that I had a good lawyer.'

'Maybe part of it was the unusual relationship,' I said helpfully. 'You know what I mean. It isn't all that common to grow up with a foster mother, instead of your real mother.'

That was greeted with such a dead silence that I wondered if I should just shut up for the rest of dinner. There were meaningful glances exchanged.

'Yes, that might have been part of it. Anyway, within three years of your leaving for Mercury, I knew I couldn't take it. I should have gone with you. I was only a child, but even then I wanted to come with you.' She looked appealingly at Dorothy, who was studying the table. Jubilant had stopped eating.

'Maybe I'd better not talk about it.'

To my surprise, Dorothy agreed. That clinched it for me. They wouldn't talk about it because they were keeping something from me

Jubilant took a nap after dinner. She said she wanted to go to the grotto with me but had to rest from the gravity. While she slept I tried once more to get Dorothy to tell me the whole story of her life on the moon.

'But *why* am I alive at all? You say you left Jubilant, your own child, three years old, with a friend who would take care of her in Luna. Didn't you *want* to take her with you?'

She looked at me tiredly. We'd been over this ground before.

'Timmy, you're an adult now, and have been for three years. I've told you that you're free to leave me if you want. You will soon, anyway. But I'm not going into it any further.'

'Mom, you know I can't insist. But don't you have enough respect for me not to keep feeding me that story? There's more behind it.'

'Yes! Yes, there is more behind it. But I prefer to let it lie in the past. It's a matter of personal privacy. Don't you have enough respect for *me* to stop grilling me about it?' I had never seen her this upset. She got up and walked through the wall and down the hill. Halfway down she started to run.

I started after her, but came back after a few steps. I didn't know what I'd say to her that hadn't already been said.

We made it to the grotto in easy stages. Jubilant was feeling much better after her rest, but still had trouble on some of the steep slopes.

I hadn't been to the grotto for four lightyears and hadn't played in it for longer than that. But it was still a popular place with the kids. There were scores of them.

We stood on a narrow ledge overlooking the quicksilver pool, and this time Jubilant was really impressed. The quicksilver pool is at the bottom of a narrow gorge that was blocked off a long time ago by a quake. One side of the gorge is permanently in shade, because it faces north and the sun never gets that high in our latitude. At the bottom of the gorge is the pool; twenty metres across, a hundred metres long, and about five metres deep. We *think* it's that deep, but just try sounding a pool of mercury. A lead weight sinks through it like thick molasses, and just about everything else floats. The kids had a fair-sized boulder out in the middle, using it for a boat.

That's all pretty enough, but this was retrograde summer, and the temperature was climbing towards the maximum. So the mercury was near the boiling point, and the whole area was thick with the vapour. When the streams of electrons from the sun passed through the vapour, it lit up, flickering and swirling in a ghostly indigo storm. The level was down, but it would never all boil away because it kept condensing on the dark cliffside and running back into the pool.

'Where does it all come from?' Jubilant asked, when she got her breath.

'Some of it's natural, but the majority comes from the factories in the port. It's a by-product of some of the fusion processes that they can't find any use for, and so they release it into the environment. It's too heavy to drift away, and so during darkyear it condenses in the valleys. This one is especially good for collecting it. I used to play here when I was younger.'

She was impressed. There's nothing like it on Luna. From what I hear, Luna is plain dull on the outside. Nothing moves for billions of years.

'I never saw anything so pretty. What do you do in it, though? Surely it's too dense to swim in?'

'Truer words were never spoken. It's all you can do to force your hand half a metre into the stuff. If you could balance, you could stand on it and sink in just about fifteen centimetres. But that doesn't mean you can't swim, you swim *on* it. Come on down, I'll show you.'

She was still gawking at the ionized cloud, but she followed me. That cloud can hypnotize you. At first you think it's all purple; then you start seeing other colours out of the corners of your eyes. You can never see them plainly, they're too faint. But they're there. It's caused by local impurities of other gases.

I understand people used to make lamps using ionized gases: neon, argon, mercury, and so forth. Walking down into quicksilver gully is exactly like walking into the glow of one of those old lamps.

Halfway down the slope, Jubilant's knees gave way. Her suit field stiffened with the first impact when she landed on her behind and started to slide. She was a rigid statue by the time she plopped into the pool, frozen into an awkward posture trying to break her fall. She slid across the pool and came to rest on her back.

I dived on to the surface of the pool and was easily carried all the way across to her. She was trying to stand up and finding it impossible. Presently she began to laugh, realizing that she must look pretty silly.

'There's no way you're going to stand up out here. Look, here's how you move.' I flipped over on my belly and started moving my arms in a swimming motion. You start with them in front of you, and bring them back to your sides in a long circular motion. The harder you dig into the mercury, the faster you go. And you keep going until you dig your toes in. The pool is frictionless.

Soon she was swimming along beside me, having a great time. Well, so was I. Why is it that we stop doing so many fun things when we grow up? There's nothing in the solar system like swimming on mercury. It was coming back to me now, the sheer pleasure of gliding along on the mirror-bright surface with your chin ploughing up a wake before you. With your eyes just above the surface, the sensation of speed is tremendous.

Some of the kids were playing hockey. I wanted to join them, but I could see from the way they eyed us that we were too big and they thought we shouldn't be out here in the first place. Well, that was just tough. I was having too much fun swimming.

After several hours, Jubilant said she wanted to rest. I showed her how it could be done without going to the side, forming a tripod by sitting with your feet spread wide apart. That's about the only thing you can do except lie flat. Any other position causes your support to slip out from under you. Jubilant was content to lie flat.

'I still can't get over being able to look right at the sun,' she said. 'I'm beginning to think you might have the better system here. With the internal suits, I mean.'

'I thought about that,' I said. 'You loo . . . Lunarians don't spend enough time on the surface to make a force-suit necessary. It'd be too much trouble and expense, especially for children. You wouldn't believe what it costs to keep a child in suits. Dorothy won't have her debts paid off for twenty years.'

'Yes, but it might be worth it. Oh, I can see you're right that it would cost a lot, but I won't be outgrowing them. How long do they last?'

'They should be replaced every two or three years.' I scooped up a handful of mercury and let it dribble through my hands and on to her chest. I was trying to think of an indirect way to get the talk on to the subject of Dorothy and what Jubilant knew about her. After several false starts, I came right out and asked her what they had been trying not to say.

She wouldn't be drawn out.

'What's in that cave over there?' she asked, rolling over on her belly.

'That's the grotto.'

'What's in it?'

'I'll show you if you'll talk.'

She gave me a look. 'Don't be childish, Timothy. If your mother wants you to know about her life in Luna, she'll tell you. It's not my business.'

'I won't be childish if you'll stop treating me like a child. We're both adults. You can tell me whatever you want without asking my mother.'

'Let's drop the subject.'

'That's what everyone tells me. All right, go on up to the grotto by yourself.' And she did just that. I sat on the lake and glowered at everything. I don't enjoy being kept in the dark, and I especially don't like having my relatives talk around me.

I was just a little bemused to find out how important it had become to find out the real story of Dorothy's trip to Mercury. I had lived seventeen years without knowing, and it hadn't harmed me. But now that I had thought about the things she told me as a child, I saw that they didn't make sense. Jubilant arriving here had made me re-examine them. Why *did* she leave Jubilant in Luna? Why take a cloned infant instead?

The grotto is a cave at the head of the gully with a stream of quicksilver flowing from its mouth. That happens all light-year, but the stream gets more substantial during the height of summer. It's caused by the mercury vapour concentrating in the cave, where it condenses and drips off the walls. I found Jubilant sitting in the centre of a pool, entranced. The ionization glow in the caves seems much brighter than outside, where it has to compete with sunlight. Add to that the thousands of trickling streams of mercury throwing back reflections, and you have a place that has to be entered to be believed.

'Listen, I'm sorry I was pestering you. I . . .'

'Shhh.' She waved her hands at me. She was watching the drops fall from the roof to splash without a ripple into the isolated pools on the floor of the cave. So I sat beside her and watched it, too.

'I don't think I'd mind living here,' she said, after what might have been an hour.

'I guess I never really considered living anywhere else.'

She faced me, but turned away again. She wanted to read my face, but all she could see was the distorted reflection of her own.

'I thought you wanted to be a ship's captain.'

'Oh, sure. But I'd always come back here.' I was silent for another few minutes, thinking about something that had bothered me more and more lately.

'Actually, I might get into another line of work.'

'Why?'

'Oh, I guess commanding a spaceship isn't what it used to be. You know what I mean?'

She looked at me again, this time trying even harder to see my face.

'Maybe I do.'

'I know what you're thinking. Lots of kids want to be ship's captains. They grow out of it. Maybe I have. I think I was born a century too late for what I want. You can hardly find a ship any more where the captain is much more than a figurehead. The real master of the ship is a committee of computers. They handle *all* the work. The captain can't even overrule them any more.'

'I wasn't aware it had got that bad.'

'Worse. All of the passenger lines are shifting over to totally automated ships. The high-gee runs are already like that, on the theory that after a dozen trips at five gees, the crew is pretty much used up.'

I pondered a sad fact of our modern civilization : the age of romance was gone. The solar system was tamed. There was no place for adventure.

'You could go to the cometary zone,' she suggested.

'That's the only thing that's kept me going towards pilot training. You don't need a computer out there hunting for black holes. I thought about getting a job and buying passage last darkyear, when I was feeling really low about it. But I'm going to try to get some pilot training before I go.'

'That might be wise.'

'I don't know. They're talking about ending the courses in astrogation. I may have to teach myself.'

'You think we should get going? I'm getting hungry.'

'No. Let's stay here a while longer? I love this place.'

I'm sure we had been there for five hours, saying very little. I had asked her about her interest in environmental engineering and got a suprisingly frank answer. This was what she had to say about her chosen profession: 'I found after I divorced my mother that I was interested in making safe places to live. I didn't feel very safe at that time.' She found other reasons later, but she admitted that it was a need for security that still drove her. I meditated on her strange childhood. She was the only person I ever knew who didn't grow up with her natural mother.

'I was thinking about heading outsystem myself,' she said after another long silence. 'Pluto, for instance. Maybe we'll meet out there someday.'

'It's possible.'

There was a little quake; not much, but enough to start the pools of mercury quivering and make Jubilant ready to go. We were threading our way through the pools when there was a long, rolling shock, and the violet glow died away. We were knocked apart, and fell in total darkness.

'What was that?' There was the beginning of panic in her voice.

'It looks like we're blocked in. There must have been a slide over the entrance. Just sit tight and I'll find you.'

'Where are you? I can't find you. Timothy!'

'Just hold still and I'll run into you in a minute. Stay calm, just stay calm, there's nothing to worry about. They'll have us out in a few hours.'

'Timothy. I can't find you. I can't ...' She smacked me across the face with one of her hands, then was swarming all over me. I held her close and soothed her. Earlier in the day I might have been contemptuous of her behaviour, but I had come to understand her better. Besides, no one likes to be buried alive. Not even me. I held her until I felt her relax.

'Sorry.'

'Don't apologize. I felt the same way the first time. I'm glad you're here. Being buried alone is much worse than just being buried alive. Now sit down, and do what I tell you. Turn your intake valve all the way to the left. Got it? Now we're using oxygen at the slowest possible rate. We have to keep as still as possible so we don't heat up too much.'

'All right. What next?'

'Well, for starters, do you play chess?'

'What? Is that all? Don't we have to turn on a signal or something?'

'I already did.'

'What if you're buried solid and your suit freezes to keep you from being crushed? How do you turn it on then?'

'It turns on automatically if the suit stays rigid for more than one minute.'

'Oh. All right. Pawn to king four.'

We gave up on the game after the fifteenth move. I'm not that good at visualizing the board, and while she was excellent at it, she was too nervous to plan her game. And I was getting nervous. If the entrance was blocked with rubble as I had thought, they should have had us out in under an hour. I had practised estimating time in the dark and made it to be two hours since the quake. It must have been bigger than I thought. It could be a full day before they got around to us.

'I was surprised when you hugged me that I could touch you. I mean your skin, not your suit.'

'I thought I felt you jump. The suits merge. When you touch me, we're wearing one suit instead of two. That comes in handy, sometimes.'

We were laying side by side in a pool of mercury, arms around each other. We found it soothing.

'You mean . . . I see. You can make love with your suit on. Is that what you're saying?'

'You should try it in a pool of mercury. That's the best way.'

'We're in a pool of mercury.'

'And we don't dare make love. It would overheat us. We might need our reserve.'

She was quiet, but I felt her hands tighten behind my back.

'Are we in trouble, Timothy?'

'No, but we might be in for a long stay. You'll get thirsty by and by. Can you hold out?'

'It's too bad we can't make love. It would have kept my mind off it.'

'Can you hold out?'

'I can hold out.'

'Timothy, I didn't fill my tank before we left the house. Will that make a difference?'

I don't think I tensed, but she scared me badly. I thought about it, and didn't see how it mattered. She had used an hour's oxygen at most getting to the house, even at her stepped up cooling rate. I suddenly remembered how cool her skin had been when she came into my arms.

'Jubilant, was your suit set at maximum cooling when you left the house?'

'No, but I set it up on the way. It was so *hot*. I was about to pass out from the exertion.'

'And you didn't turn it down until the quake?'

'That's right.'

I did some rough estimations and didn't like the results. By the most pessimistic assumptions, she might not have more than about five hours of air left. At the outside, she might have twelve hours. And she could do simple arithmetic as well as I; there was no point in trying to hide it from her.

'Come closer to me,' I said. She was puzzled, because we were already about as close as we could get. But I wanted to get our intake valves together. I hooked them up and waited three seconds.

'Now our tank pressures are equalized.'

'Why did you do that? Oh, no, Timothy, you shouldn't have. It was my own fault for not being careful.'

'I did it for me, too. How could I live with myself if you died in here and I could have saved you? Think about that.'

'Timothy, I'll answer any question you want to ask about your mother.'

That was the first time she got me mad. I hadn't been angry at her oversight with the refilling of the tank. Not even about the cooling. That was more my fault than hers. I had made it a game about the cooling rate, not really telling her how important it was to maintain a viable reserve. She hadn't taken me seriously, and now we were paying for my little joke. I had made the mistake of assuming that because she was an expert at Lunar safety, she could take care of herself. How could she do that if she didn't have a realistic estimate of the dangers?

But this offer sounded like repayment for the oxygen, and you don't do that on Mercury. In a tight spot, air is always shared freely. Thanks are rude.

'*Don't* think you owe me anything. It isn't right.'

'That's not why I offered. If we're going to die down here, it seems silly for me to be keeping secrets. Does that make sense?'

'No. If we're going to die, what's the use in telling me? What good will it do me? And that doesn't make sense, either. We're not even *near* dying.'

'It would at least be something to pass the time.'

I sighed. At that time, it really wasn't important to know what I had been trying to learn from her.

'All right. Question one: Why did Dorothy leave you behind when she came here?' Once I had asked it, the question suddenly became important again.

'Because she's not our mother. I divorced our mother when I was ten.'

I sat up, shocked silly.

'Dorothy's not ... then she's ... she's my foster mother? All this time she said she was ...'

'No, she's not your foster mother, not technically. She's your father.'

'WHAT?'

'She's your father.'

'Who the hell ... *father?* What kind of crazy game is this? Who the hell ever knows who their *father* is?'

'I do,' she said, simply. 'And now you do.'

'I think you had better tell it from the top.'

She did, and it all stood up, bizarre as it was.

Dorothy and Jubilant's mother (*my* mother!) had been members of a religious sect called the First Principles. I gathered they had a lot of screwy ideas, but the screwiest one of all had to do with something called the 'nuclear family'. I don't know why they called it that, maybe because it was invented in the era when nuclear power was first harnessed. What it consisted of was a mother and a father, *both living in the same household,* and dozens of kids.

The First Principles didn't go that far: they still adhered to the One Person-One Child convention – and a damn good thing, too, or they might have been lynched instead of queasily tolerated – but they liked the idea of both biological parents living together to raise the two children.

So Dorothy and Gleam (that was her name; they were Glitter and Gleam back in Luna) 'married', and Gleam took on the female role for the first child. She conceived it, birthed it, and named it Jubilant.

Then things started to fall apart, as any sane person could have told them it would. I don't know much history, but I know a little about the way things were back on Old Earth.

Husbands killing wives, wives killing husbands, parents beating children, wars, starvation; all those things. I don't know how much of that was the result of the nuclear family, but it must have been tough to 'marry' someone and find out too late that it was the wrong someone. So you took it out on the children. I'm no sociologist, but can see that much.

Their relationship, while it may have glittered and gleamed at first, went steadily downhill for three years. It got to the point that Glitter couldn't even share the same planet with his spouse. But he loved the child and had even come to think of her as his own. Try telling that to a court of law. Modern jurisprudence doesn't even recognize the *concept* of fatherhood, any more than it would recognize the divine right of kings. Glitter didn't have a legal leg to stand on. The child belonged to Gleam.

But my mother (*foster* mother; I couldn't yet bring myself to say father) found a compromise. There was no use mourning the fact that he couldn't take Jubilant with him. He had to accept that. But he could take a piece of her. That was so. So he moved to Mercury with the cloned child, changed his sex, and brought me up to adulthood, never saying a word about First Principles.

I was calming down as I heard all this, but it was certainly a revelation. I was full of questions, and for the time, survival was forgotten.

'No, Dorothy isn't a member of the church any longer. That was one of the causes of the split. As far as I know, Gleam is the *only* member today. It didn't last very long. The couples that formed the church pretty much tore each other apart in marital strife. That was why the court granted my divorce; Gleam kept trying to force her religion on me, and when I told my friends about it, they laughed at me. I didn't want that, even at age ten, and told the court I thought my mother was crazy. The court agreed.'

'So . . . so Dorothy hasn't had her one child yet. Do you think she can still have one? What are the legalities of that?'

'Pretty cut-and-dried, according to Dorothy. The judges don't like it, but it's her birthright, and they can't deny it. She managed to get permission to have you grown because of a loophole in the law, since she was going to Mercury and would be out of the jurisdiction of the Lunar courts. The loophole was closed shortly after you left. So you and I are pretty unique. What do you think about that?'

'I don't know. I think I'd rather have a normal family. What do I say to Dorothy now?'

She hugged me, and I loved her for that. I was feeling young and alone. Her story was still settling in, and I was afraid of what my reaction might be when I digested it to its conclusion.

'I wouldn't tell her anything. Why should you? She'll probably get around to telling you before you leave for the cometary zone, but if she doesn't, what of it? What does it matter? Hasn't she been a mother to you? Do you have any complaints? Is the biological fact of motherhood all that important? I think not. I think love is more important, and I can see that was there.'

'But she's my father! How do I relate to that?'

'Don't even try. I suspect that fathers loved their children in pretty much the same way mothers did, back when fatherhood was more than just insemination.'

'Maybe you're right. I think you're right.' She held me close in the dark.

'Of course I'm right.'

Three hours later, there was a rumble and the violet glow surrounded us again.

We walked into the sunlight hand in hand. The rescue

crew was there to meet us, grinning and patting us on the back. They filled our tanks, and we enjoyed the luxury of wasting oxygen to drive away the sweat.

'How bad was it?' I asked the rescue boss.

'Medium-sized. You two are some of the last to be dug out. Did you have a hard time in there?'

I looked at Jubilant, who acted as though she had just been resurrected from the dead, grinning like a maniac. I thought about it.

'No. No trouble.'

We climbed the rocky slope, and I looked back. The quake had dumped several tons of rock into quicksilver gully. Worse still, the natural dam at the lower end had been destroyed. Most of the mercury had drained out into the broader valley below. It was clear that quicksilver grotto would never be the magic place it had been in my youth. That was a sad thing. I had loved it, and it seemed that I was leaving a lot behind me down there.

I turned my back on it and walked down towards the house and Dorothy.

The Hero as Werwolf

Gene Wolfe

Gene Wolfe is the author of two remarkable novellas The Fifth Head of Cerberus *and* The Death of Dr Island, *the latter a Nebula Award winner. Here he returns with a chilling story of an outcast in a future Eden, a world in which most of humanity has been artificially evolved to a higher state, while a few families who were judged genetically unworthy live on, making their lives as best they can on the fringes and in the dark alleys of the bright new society.*

(Oh, the spelling of 'werwolf'? It's a legitimate alternate spelling, now rarely seen and dying out. Rather like the werwolves of this story.)

Feet in the jungle that leave no mark!
Eyes that can see in the dark—the dark!
Tongue—give tongue to it! Hark! O Hark!
Once, twice and again!

RUDYARD KIPLING
'Hunting Song of the Seeonee Pack'

An owl shrieked, and Paul flinched. Fear, pavement, flesh. death, stone, dark, loneliness and blood made up Paul's world; the blood was all much the same, but the fear took several forms, and he had hardly seen another human being in the four years since his mother's death. At a night meeting in the park he was the red-cheeked young man at the end of the last row, with his knees together and his scrupulously clean hands (Paul was particularly careful about his nails) in his lap.

The speaker was fluent and amusing; he was clearly conversant with his subject – whatever it was – and he pleased his audience. Paul, the listener and watcher, knew many of the words he used; yet he had understood nothing in the past hour and a half, and sat wrapped in his stolen cloak and his own thoughts, seeming to listen, watching the crowd and the park – this, at least, was no ghost-house, no trap: the moon was up, nightblooming flowers scented the park air, and the trees lining the paths glowed with self-generated blue light; in the city, beyond the last hedge, the great buildings new and old were mountains lit from within.

Neither human nor master, a policeman strolled about the fringes of the audience, his eyes bright with stupidity. Paul could have killed him in less than a second, and was enjoying a dream of the policeman's death in some remote corner of his mind even while he concentrated on seeming to be one of *them*. A passenger rocket passed just under the stars, trailing luminous banners.

The meeting was over and he wondered if the rocket had in some way been the signal to end it. The masters did not use time, at least not as he did, as he had been taught by the thin woman who had been his mother in the little house she had made for them in the turret of a house that was once (she said) the Gorous' – now only a house too old to be destroyed. Neither did they use money, of which he like other old-style *Homo sapiens* still retained some racial memory, as of a forgotten god – a magic once potent that had lost all force.

The masters were rising, and there were tears and laughter and that third emotional tone that was neither amusement nor sorrow – the silken sound humans did not possess, but that Paul thought might express content, as the purring of a cat does, or community, like the cooing of doves. The policeman bobbed his hairy head, grinning, basking in the recognition, the approval, of those who had raised him from animality. *See* (said the motion of his hands, the writhings of his body) *the clothing you have given me. How nice! I take good care of my things because they are yours. See my weapon. I perform a useful function – if you did not have me, you would have to do it yourselves.*

If the policeman saw Paul, it would be over. He was too stupid, too silly, to be deceived by appearances as his masters were. He would never dare, thinking him a master, to meet Paul's eye, but he would look into his face seeking approval, and would see not what he was supposed to see but what was there. Paul ducked into the crowd, avoiding a beautiful woman with eyes the colour of pearls, preferring to walk in the shadow of her fat escort where the policeman would not see him. The fat man took dust from a box shaped like the moon and rubbed it between his hands, releasing the smell of raspberries. It froze, and he sifted the tiny crystals of crimson ice over his shirt-front, grunting with satisfaction; then offered the box to the woman, who refused at first, only (three steps later) to accept when he pressed it on her.

They were past the policeman now. Paul dropped a few paces behind the couple, wondering if they were the ones tonight – if there would be meat tonight at all. For some, vehicles would be waiting. If the pair he had selected were among these, he would have to find others quickly.

They were not. They had entered the canyons between the buildings; he dropped farther behind, then turned aside.

Three minutes later he was in an alley a hundred metres ahead of them, waiting for them to pass the mouth. (The old trick was to cry like an infant, and he could do it well; but he had a new trick – a better trick, because too many had learned not to come down an alley when an infant cried.

The new trick was a silver bell he had found in the house, small and very old. He took it from his pocket and removed the rag he had packed around the clapper. His dark cloak concealed him now, its hood pulled up to hide the pale gleam of his skin. He stood in a narrow doorway only a few metres away from the alley's mouth.)

They came. He heard the man's thick laughter, the woman's silken sound. She was a trifle silly from the dust the man had given her, and would be holding his arm as they walked, rubbing his thigh with hers. The man's blackshod foot and big belly thrust past the stonework of the building – there was a muffled moan.

The fat man turned, looking down the alley. Paul could see fear growing in the woman's face, cutting, too slowly, through the odour of raspberries. Another moan, and the man strode forward, fumbling in his pocket for an illuminator. The woman followed hesitantly (her skirt was of flowering vines the colour of love, and white skin flashed in the interstices; a serpent of gold supported her breasts).

Someone was behind him. Pressed back against the metal door, he watched the couple as they passed. The fat man had got his illuminator out and held it over his head as he walked, looking into corners and doorways.

They came at them from both sides, a girl and an old, grey-bearded man. The fat man, the master, his genetic heritage revised for intellection and peace, had hardly time to turn before his mouth gushed blood. The woman whirled and ran, the vines of her skirt withering at her thought to give her leg-room, the serpent dropping from her breasts to strike with fangless jaws at the flying-haired girl who pursued her, then winding itself about the girl's ankles. The girl fell; but as the pearl-eyed woman passed, Paul broke her neck. For a moment he was too startled at the sight of other human beings to speak. Then he said, 'These are mine'.

The old man, still bent over the fat man's body, snapped: 'Ours. We've been here an hour and more.' His voice was the creaking of steel hinges, and Paul thought of ghost-houses again.

'I followed them from the park.' The girl, black-haired, grey-eyed when the light from the alley-mouth struck her face, was taking the serpent from around her legs – it was once more a lifeless thing of soft metal mesh. Paul picked up the woman's corpse and wrapped it in his cloak. 'You gave me no warning,' he said. 'You must have seen me when I passed you.'

The girl looked towards the old man. Her eyes said she would back him if he fought, and Paul decided he would throw the woman's body at her.

'Somebody'll come soon,' the old man said. 'And I'll need Janie's help to carry this one. We each take what we got ourselves – that's fair. Or we whip you. My girl's worth a man in a fight, and you'll find I'm still worth a man myself, old as I be.'

'Give me the picking of his body. This one has nothing.'

The girl's bright lips drew back from strong white teeth. From somewhere under the tattered shirt she wore, she had produced a long knife, and sudden light from a window high above the alley ran along the edge of the stained blade; the girl might be a dangerous opponent, as the old man claimed, but Paul could sense the femaleness, the woman-rut from where he stood. 'No,' her father said. 'You got good clothes. I need these.' He looked up at the window fearfully, fumbling with buttons.

'His cloak will hang on you like a blanket.'

'We'll fight. Take the woman and go away, or we'll fight.'

He could not carry both, and the fat man's meat would be tainted by the testicles. When Paul was young and there had been no one but his mother to do the killing, they had sometimes eaten old males; he never did so now. He slung the pearl-eyed woman across his shoulders and trotted away.

Outside the alley the streets were well lit, and a few passers-by stared at him and the dark burden he carried. Fewer still, he knew, would suspect him of being what he was – he had learned the trick of dressing as the masters did, even of wearing their expressions. He wondered how the black-haired girl and the old man would fare in their ragged clothes. *They must live very near.*

His own place was that in which his mother had borne him, a place high in a house built when humans were the masters. Every door was nailed tight and boarded up; but on one side a small garden lay between two wings, and in a corner of this garden, behind a bush where the shadows were thick even at noon, the bricks had fallen away. The lower floors were full of rotting furniture and the smell of rats and mould, but high in his wooden turret the walls were still dry and the sun came in by day at eight windows. He carried his burden there and dropped her in a corner. It was important that his clothes be kept clean as the masters kept theirs, though he lacked their facilities. He pulled his cloak from the body and brushed it vigorously.

'What are you going to do with me?' the dead woman said behind him.

'Eat,' he told her. 'What did you think I was going to do?'

'I didn't know.' And then: 'I've read of you creatures, but I didn't think you really existed.'

'We were the masters once,' he said. He was not sure he still believed it, but it was what his mother had taught him. 'This house was built in those days – that's why you won't wreck it: you're afraid.' He had finished with the cloak; he hung it up and turned to face her, sitting on the bed. 'You're afraid of waking the old times,' he said. She lay slumped in the corner, and though her mouth moved, her eyes were only half open, looking at nothing.

'We tore a lot of them down,' she said.

'If you're going to talk, you might as well sit up straight.' He lifted her by the shoulders and propped her in the corner. A nail protruded from the wall there; he twisted a lock of her hair on it so her head would not loll; her hair was the rose shade of a little girl's dress, and soft but slightly sticky.

'I'm dead, you know.'

'No, you're not.' They always said this (except, sometimes, for the children) and his mother had always denied it. He felt that he was keeping up a family tradition.

'Dead,' the pearl-eyed woman said. 'Never, never, never. Another year, and everything would have been all right. I want to cry, but I can't breathe too.'

'Your kind lives a long time with a broken neck,' he told her. 'But you'll die eventually.'

'I am dead now.'

He was not listening. There were other humans in the city; he had always known that, but only now, with the sight of the old man and the girl, had their existence seemed real to him.

'I thought you were all gone,' the pearl-eyed dead woman said thinly. 'All gone long ago, like a bad dream.'

Happy with his new discovery, he said: 'Why do you set traps for us, then? Maybe there are more of us than you think.'

'There can't be many of you. How many people do you kill in a year?' Her mind was lifting the sheet from his bed, hoping to smother him with it; but he had seen that trick many times.

'Twenty or thirty.' (He was boasting.)

'So many.'

'When you don't get much besides meat, you need a lot of

it. And then I only eat the best parts – why not? I kill twice a month or more except when it's cold, and I could kill enough for two or three if I had to.' (*The girl had had a knife*. Knives were bad, except for cutting up afterwards. But knives left blood behind. He would kill for her – she could stay here and take care of his clothes, prepare their food. He thought of himself walking home under a new moon, and seeing her face in the window of the turret.) To the dead woman he said: 'You saw that girl? With the black hair? She and the old man killed your husband, and I'm going to bring her here to live.' He stood and began to walk up and down the small room, soothing himself with the sound of his own footsteps.

'He wasn't my husband.' The sheet dropped limply now that he was no longer on the bed. 'Why didn't you change? When the rest changed their genes?'

'I wasn't alive then.'

'You must have received some tradition.'

'We didn't want to. We are the human beings.'

'Everyone wanted to. Your old breed had worn out the planet; even with much better technology we're still starved for energy and raw materials because of what you did.'

'There hadn't been enough to eat before,' he said, 'but when so many changed there was a lot. So why should more change?'

It was a long time before she answered, and he knew the body was stiffening. That was bad, because as long as she lived in it the flesh would stay sweet; when the life was gone, he would have to cut it up quickly before the stuff in her lower intestine tainted the rest.

'Strange evolution,' she said at last. 'Man become food for men.'

'I don't understand the second word. Talk so I know what you're saying.' He kicked her in the chest to emphasize his point, and knocked her over, he heard a rib snap ... She did not reply, and he lay down on the bed. His mother had told him there was a meeting place in the city where men gathered on certain special nights – but he had forgotten (if he had ever known) what those nights were.

'That isn't even metalanguage,' the dead woman said, 'only children's talk.'

'Shut up.'

After a moment he said: 'I'm going out. If you can make your body stand, and get out of here, and get down to the ground floor, and find the way out, then you may be able to tell someone about me and have the police waiting when I come back.' He went out and closed the door, then stood patiently outside for five minutes.

When he opened it again, the corpse stood erect with her hands on his table, her tremors upsetting the painted metal circus figures he had had since he was a child – the girl acrobat, the clown with his hoop and trained pig. One of her legs would not straighten. 'Listen,' he said, 'you're not going to do it. I told you all that because I knew you'd think of it yourself. They always do, and they never make it. The farthest I've ever had anyone get was out of the door and to the top of the steps. She fell down them, and I found her at the bottom when I came back. You're dead. Go to sleep.'

The blind eyes had turned towards him when he began to speak, but they no longer watched him now. The face, which had been beautiful, was now entirely the face of a corpse. The cramped leg crept towards the floor as he watched, halted, began to creep downward again. Sighing, he lifted the dead woman off her feet, replaced her in the corner, and went down the creaking stairs to find the black-haired girl.

'There has been quite a few to come after her,' her father said, 'since we come into town. Quite a few.' He sat in the back of the bus, on the rearmost seat that went completely across the back like a sofa. 'But you're the first ever to find us here. The others, they hear about her, and leave a sign at the meetin'.'

Paul wanted to ask where it was such signs were left, but held his peace.

'You know there ain't many folks at *all* any more,' her father went on. 'And not many of *them* is women. And *damn few* is young girls like my Janie. I had a fella here that wanted her two weeks back – he said he hadn't had no real woman in two years; well, I didn't like the way he said *real*, so I said what did he do, and he said he fooled around with what he killed, sometimes, before they got cold. You never did like that, did you?'

Paul said he had not.

'How'd you find this dump here?'

'Just looked around.' He had searched the area in ever-widening circles, starting at the alley in which he had seen the girl and her father. They had one of the masters' cold boxes to keep their ripe kills in (as he did himself), but there was the stink of clotted blood about the dump nonetheless. It was behind a high fence, closer to the park than he would have thought possible.

'When we come, there was a fella living here. Nice fella, a German. Name was Curtain – something like that. He went sweet on my Janie right off. Well, I wasn't too taken with having a foreigner in the family, but he took us in and let us settle in the big station wagon. Told me he wanted to wed Janie, but I said no, she's too young. Wait a year, I says, and take her with my blessing. She wasn't but fourteen then. Well, one night the German fella went out and I guess they got him, because he never come back. We moved into this here bus then for the extra room.'

His daughter was sitting at his feet, and he reached a

crooked-fingered hand down and buried it in her midnight hair. She looked up at him and smiled. 'Got a pretty face, ain't she?' he said.

Paul nodded.

'She's a mite thin, you was going to say. Well, that's true. I do my best to provide, but I'm feared, and not shamed to admit to it.'

'The ghost-houses,' Paul said.

'What's that?'

'That's what I've always called them. I don't get to talk to many other people.'

'Where the doors shut on you – lock you in.'

'Yes.'

'That ain't ghosts – now don't you think I'm one of them fools don't believe in them. I know better. But that ain't ghosts. They're always looking, don't you see, for people they think ain't right. That's us. It's electricity does it. You ever been caught like that?'

Paul nodded. He was watching the delicate swelling Janie's breasts made in the fabric of her filthy shirt, and only half listening to her father; but the memory penetrated the young desire that half embarrassed him, bringing back fear. The windows of the bus had been set to black, and the light inside was dim – still it was possible some glimmer showed outside. *There should be no lights in the dump.* He listened but heard only katydids singing in the rubbish.

'They thought I was a master – I dress like one,' he said. 'That's something you should do. They were going to test me. I turned the machine over and broke it, and jumped through a window.' He had been on the sixth floor, and had been saved by landing in the branches of a tree whose bruised twigs and torn leaves exuded an acrid incense that to him was the very breath of panic still; but it had not been the masters, or the instrument-filled examination room, or the jump from the window that had terrified him, but waiting in the ghost-room while the walls talked to one another in words he could sometimes, for a few seconds, nearly understand.

'It wouldn't work for me – got too many things wrong with me. Lines in my face; even got a wart – they never do.'

'Janie could.'

The old man cleared his throat; it was a thick sound, like water in a downspout in a hard rain. 'I been meaning to talk to you about her; about why those other fellas I told you about never took her – not that I'd of let some of them: Janie's the only family I got left. But I ain't so particular I don't want to see her married at all – not a bit of it. Why, we wouldn't of come here if it weren't for Janie. When her monthly come, I said to myself, she'll be wantin' a man, and what're you goin' to do way out here? Though the country was gettin' bad anyway, I must say. If they'd of had real dogs, I believe they would have got us several times.'

He paused, perhaps thinking of those times, the lights in the woods at night and the running, perhaps only trying to order his thoughts. Paul waited, scratching an ankle, and after a few seconds the old man said: 'We didn't want to do this, you know, us Pendeltons. That's mine and Janie's name – Pendelton. Janie's Augusta Jane, and I'm Emmit J.'

'Paul Gorou,' Paul said.

'Pleased to meet you, Mr Gorou. When the time come, they took one whole side of the family. They was the Worthmore Pendeltons; that's what we always called them, because most of them lived thereabouts. Cousins of mine they was, and second cousins. We was the Evershaw Pendeltons, and they didn't take none of us. Bad blood, they said – too much wrong to be worth fixing, or too much that mightn't get fixed right, and then show up again. My ma – she's alive then – she always swore it was her sister Lillian's boy that did it to us. The whole side of his head was pushed in. You know what I mean? They used to say a cow'd kicked him when he was small, but it wasn't so – he's just born like that. He could talk some – there's those that set a high value on that – but the slobber'd run out of his mouth. My ma said if it wasn't for him we'd have got in sure. The only other thing was my sister Clara that was born with a bad eye – blind, you know, and something wrong with the lid of it too. But she was just as sensible as anybody. Smart as a whip. So I would say it's likely Ma was right. Same thing with your family, I suppose?'

'I think so. I don't really know.'

'A lot of it was die-beetees. They could fix it, but if there was other things too they just kept them out. Of course when it was over there wasn't no medicine for them no more, and they died off pretty quick. When I was young, I used to think that was what it meant: die-beetees – you died away. It's really sweetening of the blood. You heard of it?'

Paul nodded.

'I'd like to taste some sometime, but I never come to think of that while there was still some of them around.'

'If they weren't masters –'

'Didn't mean I'd of killed them,' the old man said quickly. 'Just got one to gash his arm a trifle so I could taste of it. Back then – that would be twenty aught nine, close to fifty years gone it is now – there was several I knowed that was just my age . . . What I was meaning to say at the beginning was that us Pendeltons never figured on anythin' like this. We'd farmed, and we meant to keep on, grow our own truck and breed our own stock. Well, that did for a time, but it wouldn't keep.'

Paul, who had never considered living off the land, or even

realized that it was possible to do so, could only stare at him.

'You take chickens, now. Everybody always said there wasn't nothing easier than chickens, but that was when there was medicine you could put in the water to keep off the sickness. Well, the time come when you couldn't get it no more than you could get a can of beans in those stores of theirs that don't use money or cards or anything a man can understand. My dad had two hundred in the flock when the sickness struck, and it took every hen inside of four days. You wasn't supposed to eat them that had died sick, but we did it. Plucked 'em and canned 'em – by that time our old locker that plugged in the wall wouldn't work. When the chickens was all canned, Dad saddled a horse we had then and rode twenty-five miles to a place where the new folks grew chickens to eat themselves. I guess you know what happened to him, though – they wouldn't sell, and they wouldn't trade. Finally he begged them. He was a Pendelton, and used to cry when he told of it. He said the harder he begged them the scareder they got. Well, finally he reached out and grabbed one by the leg – he was on his knees to them – and he hit him alongside the face with a book he was carryin'.'

The old man rocked backward and forward in his seat as he spoke, his eyes half closed. 'There wasn't no more seed but what was saved from last year then, and the corn went so bad the ears wasn't no longer than a soft dick. No bullets for Dad's old gun, nowhere to buy new traps when what we had was lost. Then one day just before Christmas these here machines just started tearing up our fields. They had forgot about us, you see. We threw rocks but it didn't do no good, and about midnight one come right through the house. There wasn't no one living then but Ma and Dad and brother Tom and me and Janie. Janie wasn't but just a little bit of a thing. The machine got Tom in the leg with a piece of two-by-four

– rammed the splintery end into him, you see. The rot got to the wound and he died a week after; it was winter then, and we was living in a place me and Dad built upon the hill out of branches and saplings.'

'About Janie,' Paul said. 'I can understand how you might not want to let her go – '

'Are you sayin' you don't want her?' The old man shifted in his seat, and Paul saw that his right hand moved close to the crevice where the horizontal surface joined the vertical. The crevice was a trifle too wide, and he thought he knew what was hidden there. He was not afraid of the old man, and it had crossed his mind more than once that if he killed him there would be nothing to prevent his taking Janie.

'I want her,' he said. 'I'm not going away without her.' He stood up without knowing why.

'There's been others said the same thing. I would go, you know, to the meetin' in the regular way; come back next month, and the fella'd be waitin'.'

The old man was drawing himself to his feet, his jaw outthrust belligerently. 'They'd see her,' he said, 'and they'd talk a lot, just like you, about how good they'd take care of her, though there wasn't a one brought a lick to eat when he come to call. Me and Janie, sometimes we ain't et for three, four days – they never take account of that. Now here, you look at her.'

Bending swiftly, he took his daughter by the arm; she rose gracefully, and he spun her around. 'Her ma was a pretty woman,' he said, 'but not as pretty as what she is, even if she is so thin. And she's got sense too – I don't keer what they say.'

Janie looked at Paul with frightened, animal eyes. He gestured, he hoped gently, for her to come to him, but she only pressed herself against her father.

'You can talk to her. She understands.'

Paul started to speak, then had to stop to clear his throat. At last he said: 'Come here, Janie. You're going to live with me. We'll come back and see your father sometimes.'

Her hand slipped into her shirt; came out holding a knife. She looked at the old man, who caught her wrist and took the knife from her and dropped it on the seat behind him, saying, 'You're going to have to be a mite careful around her for a bit, but if you don't hurt her none she'll take to you pretty quick. She wants to take to you now – I can see it in the way she looks.'

Paul nodded, accepting the girl from him almost as he might have accepted a package, holding her by her narrow waist.

'And when you get a mess of grub she likes to cut them up, sometimes, while they're still movin' around. Mostly I don't allow it, but if you do – anyway, once in a while – she'll like you better for it.'

Paul nodded again. His hand, as if of its own volition, had strayed to the girl's smoothly rounded hip, and he felt such desire as he had never known before.

'Wait,' the old man said. His breath was foul in the close air. 'You listen to me now. You're just a young fella and I know how you feel, but you don't know how I do. I want you to understand before you go. I love my girl. You take good care of her or I'll see to you. And if you change your mind about wanting her, don't you just turn her out. I'll take her back, you hear?'

Paul said, 'All right.'

'Even a bad man can love his child. You remember that because it's true.'

Her husband took Janie by the hand and led her out of the wrecked bus. She was looking over her shoulder, and he knew that she expected her father to drive a knife into his back.

They had seen the boy – a brown-haired, slightly freckled boy of nine or ten with an armload of books – on a corner where a small, columniated building concealed the entrance to the mono-rail, and the streets were wide and empty. The children of the masters were seldom out so late. Paul waved to him, not daring to speak, but attempting to convey by his posture that he wanted to ask directions; he wore the black cloak and scarlet-slashed shirt, the gold sandals and wide-legged black film trousers proper to an evening of pleasure. On his arm Janie was all in red, her face covered by a veil dotted with tiny synthetic bloodstones. Gem-studded veils were a fashion now nearly extinct among the women of the masters, but one that served to conceal the blankness of eye that betrayed Janie, as Paul had discovered, almost instantly. She gave a soft moan of hunger as she saw the boy, and clasped Paul's arm more tightly. Paul waved again.

The boy halted as though waiting for them, but when they were within five metres he turned and dashed away. Janie was after him before Paul could stop her. The boy dodged between two buildings and raced through to the next street; Paul was just in time to see Janie follow him into a doorway in the centre of the block.

He found her clear-soled platform shoes in the vestibule, under a four-dimensional picture of Hugo de Vries. De Vries was in the closing years of his life, and in the few seconds it took Paul to pick up the shoes and conceal them behind an aquarium of phosphorescent cephalopods, had died, rotted to dust, and undergone rebirth as a fissioning cell in his mother's womb with all the labyrinth of genetics still before him.

The lower floors, Paul knew, were apartments. He had entered them sometimes when he could find no prey on the streets. There would be a school at the top.

A confused, frightened-looking woman stood in an otherwise empty corridor, a dishevelled library book lying open at her feet. As Paul pushed past her, he could imagine Janie knocking her out of the way, and the woman's horror at the savage, exultant face glimpsed beneath her veil.

There were elevators, a liftshaft, and a downshaft, all clustered in an alcove. *The boy would not have waited for an elevator with Janie close behind him . . .*

The liftshaft floated Paul as spring-water floats a cork. Thickened by conditioning agents, the air remained a gas; enriched with added oxygen, it stimulated his whole being, though it was as viscous as corn syrup when he drew it into his lungs. Far above, suspended (as it seemed) in crystal and surrounded by the books the boy had thrown down at her, he saw Janie with her red gown billowing around her and her white legs flashing. She was going to the top, apparently to the uppermost floor, and he reasoned that the boy, having led her there, would jump into the downshaft to escape her. He got off at the eighty-fifth floor, opened the hatch to the downshaft, and was rewarded by seeing the boy only a hundred metres above him. It was a simple matter then to wait on the landing and pluck him out of the sighing column of thickened air.

The boy's pointed, narrow face, white with fear under a tan, turned up towards him. 'Don't,' the boy said. 'Please, sir, good master – ' but Paul clamped him under his left arm, and with a quick wrench of his right broke his neck.

Janie was swimming head down with the down shaft current, her mouth open and full of eagerness, and her black hair like a cloud about her head. She had lost her veil. Paul showed her the boy and stepped into the shaft with her. The hatch slammed behind him, and the motion of the air ceased.

He looked at Janie. She had stopped swimming and was staring hungrily into the dead boy's face. He said, 'Something's wrong,' and she seemed to understand, though it was possible that she only caught the fear in his voice. The hatch would not open, and slowly the current in the shaft was reversing, lifting them; he tried to swim against it but the effort was hopeless. When they were at the top, the dead boy began to talk; Janie put her hand over his mouth to muffle the sound. The hatch at the landing opened, and they stepped out on to the hundred-and-first floor. A voice from a loudspeaker in the wall said: '*I am sorry to detain you, but there is a reason to think you have undergone a recent deviation from the optimal development pattern. In a few minutes I will arrive in person to provide counselling; while you are waiting it may be useful for us to review what is meant by "optimal development". Look at the projection.*

'*In infancy the child first feels affection for its mother, the provider of warmth and food . . .*' There was a door at the other end of the room, and Paul swung a heavy chair against it, making a din that almost drowned out the droning speaker.

'*Later one's peer-group becomes, for a time, all-important – or nearly so. The boys and girls you see are attending a model school in Armstrong. Notice that no tint is used to mask the black of space above their airtent.*'

The lock burst from the doorframe, but a remotely actuated hydraulic cylinder snapped it shut each time a blow from the chair drove it open. Paul slammed his shoulder against it, and before it could close again put his knee where the shattered bolt-socket had been. A chrome-plated steel rod as thick as a finger had dropped from the chair when his blows had smashed the wood and plastic holding it; after a moment of incomprehension, Janie dropped the dead boy, wedged the rod between the door and the jamb, and slipped through. He was following her when the rod lifted, and the door swung shut on his foot.

He screamed and screamed again, and then, in the echoing silence that followed, heard the loudspeaker mumbling about education, and Janie's sobbing, indrawn breath. Through the crack between the door and the frame, the two-centimetre space held in existence by what remained of his right foot, he could see the livid face and blind, malevolent eyes of the dead boy, whose will still held the steel rod suspended in air. 'Die,' Paul shouted at him. 'Die! You're dead!' The rod came crashing down.

'*This young woman*,' the loudspeaker said, '*has chosen the profession of medicine. She will be a physician, and she says now that she was born for that. She will spend the remainder of her life in relieving the agonies of disease.*'

Several minutes passed before he could make Janie understand what it was she had to do.

'*After her five years' training in basic medical techniques, she will specialize in surgery for another three years before –*'

It took Janie a long time to bite through his Achilles tendon; when it was over, she began to tear at the ligaments that held the bones of the tarsus to the leg. Over the pain he could feel the hot tears washing the blood from his foot.

The Silent Eyes of Time

Algis Budrys

For a decade from the late 1950s to the late 1960s, Algis Budrys was one of the most accomplished writers in science fiction, producing such novels as Who? *and* Rogue Moon, *both Hugo Award nominees, and many other fine stories. He retired from science fiction writing for many years, contenting himself with reviewing the offerings of others. But no doubt while he was analysing other people's sf he was germinating ideas within himself, and in 1975 he returned to the field with several new stories, of which the most outstanding was this deceptively quiet, thoughtful novelette about what might* really *happen if someone were to invent a time machine tomorrow.*

Early on a day in the spring of 1971, Clinton Gallard walked steadily along the interminable G concourse at O'Hare International. Most of the boarding areas were still well ahead. He took his time although the Caribbean flight was near departure. In a long and taut life he had detected the rhythm of how things work, and had fallen in with it.

He was a man with a rectangular torso, of equal width at shoulders and hips, thin from the side, with markedly delicate limbs. His legs were very long. He had a narrow, blade-nosed, tanned and age-spotted head. His short, thinning, coarse white hair swirled lightly about his scalp. His pale blue eyes were made secret by the deep folds creased into the leathery flesh around them, and were set far back in their sharply distinct sockets. He moved with economy, not much disturbing the hang of his carefully cut lightweight suit, and he walked with his hands ready.

He was remembering the thick humidity in the cabins of DC-3s floundering through Appalachian thunderstorms; the little fans whirring on their mounts along the edge of the overhead baggage shelf, trying to circulate the dampness and the airsick smell; the condensation running down the windows where the lightning flashed and flashed beyond the rain-drummed wings, altogether different from the blue spitting flame at the exhaust port; the briefcase clutched securely between his ankles, the two of them journeying once again to Washington where they talked New Deal but dealt with you like Calvin Coolidge.

Then he remembered tall white ships easing out of Lower New York Bay with dance bands playing; soft yellow lights along the deck at night, and couples leaning back to smile into each other's faces with their arms around their waists; tall, cold drinks with mint sprigs and a kind of white-frosted ice, and the coast lights changing to Miami. Boys dived for coins at Nassau. In Havanah, there was a winding street of little steps; a little park on an oval terrace where a man could sit at dusk, and then saunter up the hill towards a pale yellow stucco house where music played beyond the wrought iron railings.

The woman with him, Elizabeth, had a large shoulderbag slung over her Californian-cut tan poplin jacket. She was made shorter by his height, but she was nearly six feet tall, dressed for their trip in sports slacks. Only by looking around the edges of her large-lensed sunglasses could one see the beginnings of crow's feet, before the chestnut manes of her hair enclosed her high cheekbones and framed her chin and soft mouth. Smaller and younger was what Clinton Gallard conferred upon her, and love.

'We'll be at the gate in plenty of time,' Gallard remarked in his relaxed, well-projected voice. She shortened her stride. He looked about him at Avis and motel advertisements in illuminated boxes on the concrete panelling of the concourse walls. He studied one with a critical eye. It was for the new models from AWC. 'The Expert-name in Electronics.' It was not a slogan of which he approved. Until last year, the advertising campaigns had been tagged 'First . . . Best.' He thought that was a more easily grasped assertion. And it left more room in the available space, so that the picture of the product – the handsome cabinetwork and buffed metal fascia, and the big tube with the evocative colour photograph of white boats on a blue sea – could be brought closer. If you were in a game it seemed to him, you played for every millimetre of ground.

They were passing boarding areas now. Great and small alike sat facing each other until their flight was called, ignoring each other's eyes while their knees nearly touched. It made Gallard picture muzhiks squatting beside telegraph poles along the right of way, waiting to flag the daily train on the Trans-Siberian railroad. It was not a world substantially different from the view before him when he'd sat in the valedictory chair at the Warton School of Finance back in 1928.

As they neared their gate, he said, 'Shit!' Elizabeth raised her head like a doe.

Gallard stopped and they waited for the man hurrying towards them. He was fifty-eight, sixty, faced like a beagle, cyanotic at the lips, wet-combed under his Homburg. 'Clint! I'm glad I didn't miss you! I've been waiting for you.' He thrust his hand forward, and Gallard took it in a measured grip.

'How are you, Charles,' he said pleasantly. 'Mr Treville, this is Miss Farrier. Elizabeth, Mr Treville is the president of AWC Electronics.' His successor. A man who had come up through the sales department.

'Very pleased to meet you, Miss Farrier,' Treville said, barely diverting his glance from Gallard. 'Clint, may we please ask you to postpone your trip?'

Gallard raised his eyebrows.

'Clint –' Treville looked about them. 'Please come and let me talk to you.'

Gallard studied him briefly. He sucked in one corner of his lower lip. Then he smiled in a kindly manner.

'Elizabeth,' he said, 'would you please see to cancelling our seats and all that? I doubt if you'll be able to retrieve our baggage this late. But I'm sure Mr Treville took that imposition into account and made his request nonetheless. Please meet us in the V.I.P. lounge.' He pressed her shoulder fondly. 'Don't worry – you won't be long, and I'll be surrounded by other old gaffers. We know what to do for each other.'

He turned away with Treville. 'It's strange to see you alone, Charlie,' he remarked as they made their way back up to the concourse. 'No assistants carrying relevant papers, no vice-presidents to part the waves for you.'

'Christ almighty, Clint, I had a bitch of a time catching you! By the time I got your housekeeper to admit where you might be, I had to just grab a cab and hustle out here. It's important, Clint. Here you are, all set to just sit around. Got yourself a nice little cooze there to keep off the cool breezes. And here's Charlie Treville saying "Pardon the interruption."'

'And I was telling you the point was made, Charles,' Gallard said, his eyes crinkling in a kindly manner. 'Just telling you it was made.'

He and Treville exchanged no further words between there

and the lounge. Gallard was remembering the morning when he was called in to Elmo Daugherty's old walnut-panelled office in the General Office building they'd used to have on lower Michigan Avenue. 'Clint,' Elmo Daugherty had said out of his flat, overslung mouth, 'I believe it would do the company some good if we made you a vice-president and let you straighten out that mess in Purchasing.'

Gallard had said 'The trouble in Purchasing is your cousin Paul.'

Daugherty had stood looking out of the window with his hands behind his back. 'So force my cousin Paul to resign.'

They reached a quiet table in a corner of the lounge, and the waitress took their drink orders. Gallard leaned back in his chair, extending his legs. Treville hunched forward.

'It's your boy Hessenbirger down at Churchville Research,' he said. 'This time he's opened a can of worms.' He eyed Gallard steadily. He ought to have been vindictive, perhaps triumphant. This sort of thing was presumed to be the reason why Gallard had left. Instead, Treville's mouth was slack with fear.

Gallard studied him carefully. He did not like to see fear in men of Treville's type. They always tried to make you pay, later, for having seen it. They operated along simple lines.

Gallard visualized a structure, called AWC, made of intricately curved wires. He saw it floating silvery and highlighted against a featureless soft black background. Because the wires looped and intercurved, they appeared to define and enclose a certain volume of space like a Tchelitchew sculpture. It was possible to misconstrue the space for the sculpture. In actual fact, even the wires were imaginary – a convenient representation of the tracks taken by moving particles whose courses were quite literally, careers. And if one watched very closely, one could see AWC subtly throbbing to the frictions of their passage. Whereas Treville saw nothing but the shape, and furthermore thought it was all solid inside, like a potato.

Gallard smiled. 'What has Hessenbirger done?'

'Worked up a way of reaching the future. I don't know what you'd call it – a – a *thing*! it's electronic, but it moves a man into the future and lets him bring things back – a future mass transceiver? But it works. He's brought back stuff – coins, newspapers. He handed some of them out for souvenirs. And *then* he reported he'd made this thing.'

'The future,' Gallard cocked an eyebrow. 'Really?'

'Here –' Treville handed him a U.S. quarter dated 1975.

'I'd rather see one of the newspapers,' Gallard said, turning the coin in his lean fingers. 'That would be harder to fake, I think.'

But within him he pictured a landscape of rolling meadows and wooded glades with soft afternoon sky above, and in his mind he peeled away an infinitely thin layer of nearly perfect transparency, to reveal the same landscape, which in turn he lifted away for yet another, and others, as the leaves slowly shifted and the grass deployed in lax formations, and dusk fell upon this land within his mind until, there, past many increments now, he felt the first faint onset of an evening star, only its farthermost photons yet impinging on his senses, so thin were the films.

'It's not a fake,' Treville said. 'It's been corroborated. Mangrum had him make another run. We now have calenders, news-magazines, and Polaroids of completed buildings standing on vacant lots.' Treville broke off as the waitress set down their drinks, smiled, and left.

'How many people know about it?'

'I don't know. All of Hessenbirger's associates, to begin with; he bragged to them as soon as he'd got back. Then a girl file clerk on her way to Mangrum's office – Hessenbirger's got a yen for her, I suppose, and wanted to impress her. Then a draughtsman named Pogrobius; Hessenbirger likes to chase around the strip joints with him on Friday nights, and he happened to bump into him in the stairwell. Then Mangrum, of course – after all, you've got to let your Manager of Engineering know about it sometime, right? Then Mangrum called me, and sent a messenger with a confidential envelope of reports and samples, and I've spoken to Elmo Daugherty.'

Daugherty was Chairman of the Board. A wise old fat man. Wary. 'What did Elmo say?'

'He said to get hold of you.'

'When did you speak to him?'

'This morning. I've been waiting for Mangrum to confirm everything. It's been twenty-four hours.'

'Is anything specific in writing?'

'Sure. Engineering memos, research notes, and a slew of paper from Mangrum. Corporations have paper brain cells.' Treville picked up his glass and drained off a mouthful. 'You know that.'

Gallard waved to Elizabeth across the room. 'You do need me after all, Charles,' he agreed. 'I'll go see Elmo. Meanwhile, please arrange for a complete presentation to me at Churchville tomorrow morning. Ask Mangrum to meet me in the bar at the Marriott at seven this evening. Oh, and I'll need two connecting single rooms, and two seats on the Churchville plane. I suppose Mangrum can have his secretary do that for us.'

'It's like you'd never left,' Treville said quietly.

'Don't worry, Charles – I'll get it done and go away again.'

'You had a lot of good ideas, Clint. Sitting where I sit these days, I can really appreciate what it must have taken to build up the company the way you did. There are lots of times when I wish –'

'And this is one of the times,' Gallard said with a cordial smile. 'But I *will* go away again. Promise.'

Treville began to say something else, and then said: 'I'll come on the early morning flight.'

'Well, of course you'd want to be at the presentation,' Gallard said agreeably. He sipped his sherry. He thought to himself. 'What does it say in tomorrow's newspaper, Charles?'

Treville shook his head, blurring his pale features. 'You wouldn't believe it. You'll see for yourself. I wouldn't want to discuss things like that. The future is about people we're doing business with *now*, you know? How can I discuss it?'

Gallard looked at him kindly. 'All right, Charles. If you can't say something good, don't say anything at all.'

Here she was.

'Sit down, Elizabeth,' Gallard said. 'We'll be going to a place called Churchville, Indiana, tonight.' He signalled to the waitress for her, thinking of Elizabeth systematically emptying the shoulderbag into the drawers of an Indiana motel credenza; the sun lotions and bathing attire in one drawer, the pills and ampules and syringes into another. She would come to him in the night from the next bed if she heard him gasping; she would slip the nitroglycerin tablet tenderly under his tongue. 'Chivas on the rocks with a splash of soda and a twist of lemon for the lady,' he told the waitress softly.

He handed the girl his credit card. 'We'll be leaving after that, so we'd like a check, please, as well.' He raised his hand and gestured away Charles Treville's hasty move towards his own wallet. 'No – that's all right, Charles. I'll be sending in a consultation bill.' He winked the wink of one old travelling salesman to another, a thing he had studied many times. The thing was, though, that Treville inalterably saw him as a cutthroat, as if in a Travelodge mirror. So all the amenities between them were *pro forma*, and it did not actually matter which format one selected. Gallard sipped his sherry with a tender little smile.

2

Elizabeth drove their rental car to Daugherty's home in Lake Forest, Gallard sat with his head resting comfortably on his seat-back, his arms around his knees.

The day had come when Daugherty had asked him to dine alone with the fattening old man in the upstairs room of the new G.O. 'Clint, you son of a bitch,' Daugherty had said. 'I don't see any way to avoid making you chief operating officer. I'm gonna settle down on the board and go buy myself some big stone resting place on the North Shore, there, and let you make me richer.'

They pulled up on the bluestone apron at the front of the landside entrance and went up the stone steps together at Gallard's most comfortable pace. Gallard rang, and the butler's eyes widened when he saw who it was, but he murmured 'Very nice to see you here again, Mr Gallard,' as to the manner born.

Elmo Daugherty grunted when they came into the room. 'Sit down, Clint. Drink? Miss Farrier? No and no.' The three of them sat there in the library, Elizabeth in a corner turning the pages of a book, Gallard and Daugherty in two chairs near each other at the fireplace. 'What do you know so far, Clint?' the old man said.

'As much as Charlie knows.'

'Well, that's about as much as I know. What do you think?'

'I think Hessenbirger's done it. The same way he's done everything else. He sat there playing with his mind, and took a snatch of something he'd read in somebody's paper, and something he'd rubbed up against at a symposium, and something he'd dreamed when he was a kid, and the next thing he knew, he had a soldering iron in his hand.'

'Son of a bitch, Clint, how do people do that?'

'That same way you don't have to read the stock tables. The tables are for technicians. Like high school civics texts. The purpose of college is to refute their lies and substitute a more sophisticated set. Meanwhile, people are out running the world.'

'Well, Hessenbirger sure as hell doesn't run the world.'

'He's just turned it upside down, Elmo. *That's* the point.'

'I know what the fucking point is!' Daugherty glanced quickly towards a tranquil Elizabeth and jerked his head back into place again. 'We've got a nice, viable thing going here; big share of the market, control of half the basic patents –'

'Thanks to Hessenbirger.'

'Thanks to you for finding Hessenbirger. – Bigger share of the market than we deserve, nice chunk of licensing income, lots of O.E.M. parts sales. We're not golden, but we're a fuck of a lot better off than anybody else in this country. We could have been up shit creek with the rest of them. You really built something, Clint. But you built it around one man –'

'Around an approach. One man happens to fit it superbly at this point in the company's history. But there can always be others, as long as we keep the approach. You create a climate, and the sun shines.'

'Yeah, well, we've got ourselves a tornado now. You'd better get us out of it.'

Gallard stared calmly into the fire flickering amid the gas logs. 'Why?' He smiled slightly to himself.

'Because you know damned well this isn't some lousy little policy question you and I can knock heads over and it hardly matters who wins. This is the whole world going to hell. Shit – you know what people are like. Get rich quick. Take the money and run. Crooked as a ram's horn. Cinch bettors. We've got our society surrounded and infiltrated with security systems out the ying-yang, and you still get pilferage and embezzlement being national industries. That's what they'd do, man – steal from the future and never think twice about it. Charles Treville even had a couple of minutes where he wondered if we couldn't market this thing! Jesus!'

'Why me? I'm out of it, Elmo. Shot down.'

'My ass. You quit. And I know damned well why you quit, and I don't blame you. My old man went down the hall flat on his back on a stretcher, right past all the secretaries and janitors, on his eighth and last coro-fucking-nary, and by God they had to pry a piece of correspondence out of his hand in the ambulance. I get my check-up every month, and when some of those smart La Salle Street Money boys want me for something, you can bet your sweet patutie they come out here; it's just as easy to foam at the mouth and die in the back of a limousine as it is in some Goddamned North Western Railway commuter car. But don't give me that shot-down crap. I know whose balls I've got in my pocket and the count sure doesn't include yours. You had me pinned to the mat.' Suddenly Daugherty chuckled. 'Too bad.'

Gallard said pleasantly: 'I think it was Bobby Layne of the Detroit Lions who said he never lost – there were just days when he ran out of time.'

'Yeah, well, time's got you some extra time, Clint, boy.'

'I see. Nobody else can handle Hessenbirger.'

'Any two-year-old named Clinton Sturges Gallard could have figured that out by now. No – no, he's got us by the short hair, all right, but that's not all of it.' Daugherty brooded. Gallard watched him carefully. The fat man drew dignity about him like a sheik donning a caftan over a belly-band full of skinning knives.

'Maybe –' Daugherty stopped, considered, proceeded. 'You know, you've been right many times. You said the Japs would come, and they did. You pumped up Churchville and got

Hessenbirger in there. Now we purchase what we want from our Far Eastern colleagues, but some of it's our own property under licence. And we're still building and selling over here. You take a look at where some of the other outfits are, and you have to say to yourself that Clint Gallard kept AWC's ass out of the bucket. I have to sit here and think about a track record like that.' Daugherty nodded to himself. 'I do. All right, but then Charlie Treville and the other boys in Sales began getting their back up. Every time you set a sales target, what I heard was a lot of screaming about how we couldn't meet competition on dealer profit margins and product reliability. They told me the dealers were fomenting about too much warranty work against low per-unit income. And they had a point. We were costing too high at the factories. But maybe that *was* Manufacturing's fault.'

He'd spent years attempting to introduce efficiency into the factories. The managers always agreed enthusiastically that it was time to take a new look at how things were done. And then they'd settle for whatever good old Joe, the senior production engineer, told them. If you looked too closely at good old Joe, with his twenty years in towards his pension, maybe somebody'd think good old Manager wasn't untouchable either. But if you all stuck together and waited it out, and formed little alliances with Charlie Treville's people, why, something might happen to get that son of a bitch Gallard off everybody's back. So they met their cost targets by cutting quality. And Marketing made up for it by proving it was time to raise the advertising budget. It was the good old difference between the way business is talked and the way business is done. 'American Wireless Corporation is a third-generation company, Elmo,' Gallard said. 'We're not like the postwar organizations. Now don't tell me you're just realizing how the game is played, Coach.'

Daugherty waved his hand. 'All right, all right, I know

what it's like to get your heel tendons nibbled in the dark. That comes with the territory. Any time you want to bitch about this being a mossback outfit, just remember you didn't do badly in it. And it let you attract people like Hessenbirger, and this hotshot Cadwallader you've got managing the microwave plant, and Austin over in O.E.M. Sales, Rickard in Paris Merchandising, and half a dozen other monkeys you've got climbing up all the ladders we've got. Don't wave that tarbrush around so fast and loose. I remember when if we'd let you have your way, every colour TV in America would have that damn filter wheel rumbling around in front of the screen.' He chuckled again. 'There's a Moscow for every Napoleon. That's why corporations like committee decisions. But sometimes ...'

He paused for a long while. 'I've wondered if you see this company the same way I do,' he mused. 'I don't think many people do.'

'Really?'

'I've been with it, one way or another, almost from the beginning. That's – what? – forty-six years. I was one of the first employees that wasn't a partner. Came up through the Comptroller's Department, just like you did. Shit, I *was* the Comptroller's Department for a while.' The stubby-fingered hand came down hard on the arm of the chair.

'I'm aware of that, Elmo,' Gallard said. In the last year of his tenure, the senior accountants had begun producing policy memos against maintaining in-house development, and in favour of subcontracting major assemblies. 'I'm always interested in what could make my own people turn against me.'

'Yeah, well, maybe I was interested in what you'd come up with instead. I figured a smart operator like you could cook out alternate solutions and still meet the profit targets I promised the stockholders. Too bad you never quite had the time.'

'You were getting ready to tell me about something else, Elmo.'

'Yeah. Yeah. I was. I was going to say a corporation is one of the world's crudest life-forms. It feeds on its market, and it develops size in response to intake volume, you know? It gets its shape from the constituents in what it eats. So it gets big, and puts out new pseudopods and retracts old ones, and that looks like evolution. But it doesn't really have any organs. The people in it know they're not an arm or a heart. They're just a piece of pseudopod. And for all they know, they may be getting vestigial. So they're always looking around for hostility. They've always got their heads up in case something says it's time to slough them off.' Daugherty stroked his hand ruminatively along his jaw.

'A corporation gets no poontang, you know?' he said. 'Doesn't reproduce. We talk about twenty thousand independent businessmen in our dealer network, and we point to a dozen subsidiaries, but it's all pseudopods. Feed momma ipecac and the children vomit. A corporation only gets one life. So it's got to live forever. To do that, it has to keep changing shape. Got to have people who might be cancer, but might be a new chromosome, too. Might be the only kind of mutation we can get, you know?'

Gallard smiled pleasantly. 'Elmo, I told Charlie Treville and I'm sure he promptly told you. I will go to Churchville, I will straighten things out. There's no need to motivate me.'

'Yeah, well, I like to be subtle. I'm a ham-fisted Irishman from Tulsa and I like to be subtle.'

Daugherty faced forward again. 'Time,' he said. 'Paradoxical, its being time. The kettle everything boils down in.'

Riding to Meigs Field for the commuter airline, Gallard watched the limbs of the elms along Sheridan Road form traceries overhead, their outermost shoots barely misted with the first tentative green buddings of spring. 'Elizabeth,' he remarked, 'did you know that the head of one of America's top twenty companies thinks of his product as excrement?'

3

The Beech 99 put them down on the south side of the city, miles from the Marriott, which was located near the industries on the north-east side. Riding through it in the taxi with Elizabeth, Gallard looked around him at Churchville. It was an old riverfront town that had spread, mainly in the nineteenth century, and presented a variety of architectural styles in wood and brick. It had been founded in 1794, when the United States of America had sent General Anthony Wayne here to stand against the last vestiges of commercial encroachment by the French. Situated to take advantage of barge traffic, crossed, eventually, by railroads connecting with Chicago and St Louis and the Mississippi, made an Interstate intersection by the Federal Highway Act of the 1950s, it had a population of 150,000 and an industrial capacity outstripping the gross national product of many civilized nations.

He looked over at a riverfront section that had been condemned, was partially wrecked, and was dotted with fresh signs promising office occupancy in the Indian Life Tower Complex in the spring of next year. Gallard could remember when there had been an old drummers hotel there, with photographs of twelve-wheeled steam engines in the bar, and cold draught beer in thick, seamed balloon glasses. There was still one block, away from the renewal area, where all the shops were in 1870 decor or its approximation, and the gas-lighted street was red brick. But it was a tourist development, ten years old, sponsored by the Chamber of Commerce.

'I wonder, Elizabeth – are you aware of the long-term effects of the Louisiana Purchase?' he almost said. Instead, he sat back as the dusk gathered.

They passed a strip shopping development; a grocery store, a fried chicken place, a beauty salon and a TV repair. 'Genuine AWC Parts,' the decal said. And if the dealer was bright enough to count, he was using them in everything that came into his shop. A Zenith ran just as well on an AWC replacement tube as it did on original equipment, and the dealer's profit was a hell of a lot higher. Gallard's lower teeth touched his upper lip.

Shortly after he had seen the first star, they reached the motel. They checked in with the usual amount of 'Yes, Mr Gallard', and promises of delivery if their baggage caught up, and after they had refreshed themselves as well as possible, they made a dinner reservation for eight o'clock and went down to the bar to wait for Mangrum.

Gallard had always considered this bar a likeable fraud. Dressed in beams and siding taken from old farm buildings and refinished in plastic sprays to look unfinished, it gave him a feeling of coziness which the dim cocktail candles on each table made even more appropriate. A girl with a guitar was singing quietly beside the stone fireplace, seated on a high stool and wearing a gingham dress, blonde hair long and clean in the light from a baby spot as she bent her head gracefully towards the microphone.

They made their way towards a table that would let him see the parking lot entrance, and sat down. He settled himself comfortably and smiled at Elizabeth. 'Shall we both have another?' he asked. She smiled back at him, her eyes almost the same colour as his, now that her glasses were put away in the bag, and he winked at her.

A waitress came over, dressed in the standard short, low-cut costume, and he smiled up at her pleasant face.

'May I bring you a drink sir?'

'Yes, thank you. You're new since my last time here, aren't you? This is Elizabeth, and I'm Clint. What's your name?'

'Patty, sir,' she smiled back.

'Clint. My father's name was Sir. Well, Patty, please bring Elizabeth a Chivas on the rocks, with a splash and a twist, and I'll have a dry sherry, straight up. You mustn't bring me any more after that, because I might embarrass Elizabeth, but there'll be another gentleman joining us shortly.'

The girl's smile widened by the extent he'd been hoping for. 'All right, Clint, we'll do all that. Can I bring you some cheese and crackers to get on with?'

'That would be very nice. Thank you.' He watched her walk away towards the service bar, his eyes resting on the play of candlelight upon the sheer dark nylon over her thighs. He let the singer's music wash away all his thinking while he leaned back in the chair. My soldiers lie slain for the emperor's head, he mused. Huzzah for the monarch; a mass for the dead.

Patty brought them their drinks and a snack, bending low over the table to set them down. 'What's that perfume?' he asked, and when she told him, with pleasure, he remarked: 'It's very nice. Thank you, Patty.' He pushed the snack towards Elizabeth's side of the table and sipped his drink slowly, watching people come and go, and Patty and the other waitress circulating among the tables, bending, stooping, reaching, exchanging pleasantries with the clientele. When the singer finished her set he applauded softly. After a while, he saw Harry Mangrum come in. He smiled towards the man and raised one arm in the air.

When Gallard had been managing the old Akron plant that was now a regional parts depot, his assistant had been a man named Frank Childress who loved to organize touch football games at the company July picnic. He would raise his hand in the air, and drop it to send his runners forward before he passed off, but he could not bring himself to touch Gallard if Gallard intercepted and ran near him. Not even if he ran at him. Gallard lowered his arm, remembering Childress sitting on the grass with his hand over his bloody mouth, still not claiming a touch.

Mangrum was a spare, short man with protruding jaw muscles and a downswept mouth. He wore bifocals and brushed his hair straight back. His clothes were tight. He came over with short quick steps. His handshake was bony.

Gallard introduced him to Elizabeth and Mangrum acknowledged her stiffly. He sat down with his hands one atop the other on the table.

'I appreciate your taking the time away from your family this evening,' Gallard said to him. The man nodded. When Patty came over, he ordered a tomato juice.

'It's an important thing,' Mangrum said, clipping out each syllable. 'We'll have all the facts for you in the morning.'

'I'm sure you will. I just want to get the feel of the situation tonight. Tell me – what security measures have you taken?'

Mangrum glanced uncomfortably towards Elizabeth.

'No – no, that's all right. I'm Miss Farrier's only interest in this situation. Please go ahead with the details.'

Mangrum clasped his hands more tightly. 'All right, if you say so. The first thing I did was identify everybody Hessenbirger had talked to. Then I got them all up to my office right away. I reminded them this thing is just as much AWC's property as anything else from our labs, and I told them the company had a right to expect confidentiality.'

Gallard nodded. 'Sound practice. Who is "everybody"?'

'Four research engineers, a draughtsman, and a girl file clerk. And I hadn't let Hessenbirger leave my office after he'd told me.'

'And that contained the situation?'

Mangrum shook his head. 'No. Not all the way. When I asked them, it turned out the girl had shown a 1973 dime to the secretarial pool she worked with. There were eight in the pool, plus the supervisor.'

'And how did you solve that?'

'Delayed it, first. I called the supervisor and told her to move the whole bunch into the first floor conference room and wait for me. Then I called one of my assistants and sent him there to keep them company until I was free.'

'How much do you suppose your assistant learned from the experience?'

'It can't have been very much. And he's been with me for a long time; he's learned to keep his guesses to himself until called for.'

'And what else did you do to handle that offshoot?'

'When I could, I went down there and apologized for keeping them after work. I told them I'd authorize overtime pay. I sent my assistant home, and then I told the girls I'd met somebody at a Rotary luncheon who made a passing remark to me about some defence work that had gone through the labs recently. And I said I'd traced the leak back to this particular secretarial pool.'

Gallard smiled. 'Go on.'

'I made the point that we like to operate on the basis that "What you see here, what you hear here, let it stay here." We like to feel all our employees understand that. I said that the trained government security investigators I'm often in contact with always made the point that it wasn't just deliberate malice or espionage they were constantly checking for – it was simple gossip. I said that gossip isn't against the law, but the results can be. And I said I felt it was time to caution this particular group.'

'You said all that.'

'Yes, sir. I had the conference room microphones on. You can hear the tape tomorrow, if you'd like to.'

'That won't be necessary. Go on.'

'I said I wanted each of them to privately examine their consciences and see if they hadn't been looking forward to telling somebody about our demonstration coin. And I said I hoped they understood this example for what it was – a step taken by the company to teach a valuable lesson without singling out any particular individuals at this time. And I said a note was being put in each of their folders in Personnel to show they had attended this conference and had the benefit of this lesson. I pointed out that this was better than giving one single person a bad reference that would terminate them at AWC and make them unemployable anywhere else in Churchville.'

Gallard said: 'And how did they take to that?'

Mangrum's lips turned upwards momentarily. 'They got the message.'

'Very intelligently done, Harry. And what did you do about the primary contacts?'

'Well, I took care of that as best I could before I fixed the secretaries. First, I got the dime back from the clerk and I got the newspaper entertainment pages from the draughtsman.'

'Did you tell *them* it was a hoax?'

Mangrum shook his head. 'No. Hessenbirger would have contradicted me. And the engineers knew he'd come up with something that wasn't a coin die or a printing press.'

'Had they seen him operate it?'

'No. He has his own area in the labs, and they stay out of it. You know what he's like. They look in once in a while, of course.'

'Has anyone seen him operate it?'

Mangrum nodded. 'Yes. I have. But that was later.'

'I didn't mean to make you digress, Harry. Go on.'

'After I got the evidence away from them, I told them all to stay ready for detail meetings with the brass. That got the four engineers to thinking the right way.'

'Very good, Harry. That leaves the file clerk and the draughtsman. What about them?'

'They're in single rooms at a motel. So's Hessenbirger. With another one of my assistants.'

'How do they explain that to their families?'

'None of the three of them are married. The girl doesn't live at home.'

'Fortunate. Well – I suppose you had your secretary take down a transcript of the meeting in your office?'

Mangrum nodded. 'Yes. I enclosed a copy with my sealed report to Mr Treville.'

'How many copies are there?'

'They're all confidential.'

'I understand that, Harry. Kept in locked filing cabinets and all that. How many, however?'

'One for Mr Treville, one for the office confidential files, one copy for the legal department – they'll make a Xerox, of course, so they can divide it between their general files and the patent section – and I have a personal confidential file.'

'Five, plus the Xero.'

'Four, plus.'

'Your secretary will have kept a carbon, I think, clipped to the pages from her shorthand book. In case anyone ever questions her accuracy.'

Mangrum frowned. 'I suppose that's right. But she'll have locked that up, too. She's a mature, level-headed woman.'

'And where are her files.'

'Well, I don't know – somewhere in the area near her desk.'

'No matter,' Gallard said easily. 'There will also be Xeroxes made of Mr Treville's copy in Chicago, I imagine.'

'I'm not responsible for anything that goes on at the General Office.'

'Quite so. Don't worry about it, Harry. Well, now, we have engineering memos and Hessenbirger's working notes, too, I suppose.'

'Being treated on the same basis.'

'Right. And your secretary doesn't discuss office matters outside.'

'She never has, or she wouldn't be working for me.'

'Yes. Now, what about this overnight business? How did you persuade Hessenbirger and the others to go along with that?'

Mangrum's lips thinned momentarily. 'He demanded a promise I'd file a report to the G.O. that would bring you down here. I gave it to him, and he persuaded the other two.'

'That's a nice compliment to your reputation for honesty.'

'I can do without his judgement.'

Gallard sighed. 'Look, Harry, Hessenbirger is simply incapable of responding maturely to anyone who directly supervises him. There is no way he's ever going to behave reasonably with you, but don't take it personally.'

'I've understood all that from the day I was hired.'

'Yes. Well – this motel where they're all staying. This would be the second night, now. Where are they? Here?'

Mangrum's head jerked. 'I don't have any budget for things like this. They're all at that motel near the manufacturing plant. It's clean and serviceable.'

'The one near Route 30? Where the truckers get rooms for six dollars a night?'

'It's the same one I was booked into when I came to interview here.'

'I didn't know that,' Gallard said. He looked at Mangrum's knuckles. 'What about Hessenbirger's device?'

'I locked up his area.'

'Is it turned off?'

'Hessenbirger says it is. And I pulled the plug out of the power supply.'

'What does his device look like?'

Mangrum grimaced. 'It's about what you'd expect – a lot of bread-boarding, and equipment racks patched in, and a station for the operator. That's just a three-sided box made out of pegboard. So he can hang things on it. And a lab stool to sit on. You'll see it tomorrow.'

'And it uses some sort of standard power supply?'

'Two twenty volts AC, right out of the wall. I don't know how many amps it draws. I had him make the one run in it before we shut everything down. Just to make sure it wasn't some kind of charade. He was gone for about twenty minutes.'

'Does the whole machine go? If it's attached to the wall?'

'No. Just he goes. And the stool. Whatever's inside the box, I suppose.'

'Does that tell you anything? What I mean to say is, I'm no engineer, of course. I wonder whether you have any thoughts on what principles he's using or how his hardware works. Have you discussed it with him?'

Mangrum sat back. 'No, sir, I haven't. I haven't read his notes, either, and I won't until I'm authorized to do that. I've instructed him to have a complete explanation in the morning.'

'Are you impressed by what he's done?'

'I'd be a fool not to be.' There was a pause. 'I'll be in the history books as the bureaucrat who didn't hand him the keys to the city.'

Gallard smiled sympathetically. 'Take an old man's word – for every historian there are two to refute him. Personally, I feel AWC was well justified in its selection of managers for Churchville.'

Mangrum nodded stiffly. 'Thank you.'

'What further plans do you have for handling these people?'

'Sir, all of that is up to you. I've done every reasonable thing I could. I've got this event confined to a practicable set of dimensions, and I've notified the GO. I didn't need Hessenbirger to tell me to do that. Now you're here. I'll devote every possible effort of Churchville Division towards carrying out your decisions and instructions. I think I've done everything anyone in my position could do, and I'm going to go on doing that. As well as carrying out all the other assignments on our schedule.'

Gallard smiled at him. 'Well said. All right, Harry. I'm looking forward to a comprehensive presentation in the morning. You'll be picking us up at seven thirty? How about a real drink before you go? Well, all right – thank you again for coming. It's been very valuable.'

They said good night and Mangrum left. Gallard shook his head. 'Would you believe,' he remarked to Elizabeth, 'that people plan and labour to achieve that man's position?' He sipped his sherry.

'Frozen sleep,' Elizabeth said.

Gallard continued to study the glass in his hand. 'Yes. You've been thinking it through. Practical applications. It would be nice to be brought forward in time and find surgeons who do heart transplants that work. Quite a bit of that sort of thing comes to mind, yes, it does. But there have been no miracles in my past, and there's no reason to expect otherwise of the future.' He grinned. 'I wonder if Mangrum gave her another dime.' He looked around him at the room.

Outposts, he thought. He remembered that in Akron the only time he ever saw the good dining-rooms was when the General Office people came to town. You'd sit there taking mental notes in your expense account, looking forward to a stiff policy memo about over-entertaining, wondering what the visiting brass would find wrong at the plant in the morning.

Gallard glanced at his wrist. 'Let us be served,' he said, and they went in to dinner. He toyed with his boiled fish. He lost interest in the lemon-dressing salad after the first few forkfuls. He remembered how he had eaten steaks here – good, hot New York cuts sizzling on platters you wouldn't dare touch – and had sat smoking a cigar and drinking Grand Marnier on the rocks, trading jokes with his staff and the Churchville management who were there to entertain them. He eyed a man at the next table piling sour cream and bacon bits on his baked potato. 'Your filet looks very good, Elizabeth,' he said politely. 'They know how to treat beef here.'

4

He sat on the edge of the bed and called Lake Forest. When the houseman had got the phone to Daugherty, Gallard said: 'I think we'll be able to manage.'

'What's the situation?'

'Well, Mangrum has been clever with the people under his thumb and successful with the rest. I give him a passing grade. I believe money and footwork will do the remainder.'

'Go ahead and spend the money. Tell Treville I said so.' Daugherty grunted. 'And supply the footwork.'

'I've been taking all that as given, Elmo. I'm calling to impress upon you that they know what we're doing. There's too much paper in existence, and too many people who'll be moved around. 1975 is sitting up there waiting for us.'

There was a pause on the line. 'I suppose I was hoping against it. But I know.'

'So the best I can do is ensure they are we.'

'Well, I hope you can attain your best.'

Gallard pictured the fat man sitting on his bed with his stomach on his thighs, his shoulders round, his head collared in the folds of his neck. A pile of Daugherty, pressed upon. Early to bed – it was nine o'clock in the Central time zone; for that matter, nine o'clock pulses beat in the wrist under Gallard's 10 PM watch, but tomorrow morning the leverage would be the other way.

'Elmo, do you see a single major commercial use for this thing?'

'I had a bunch, at first. The more I think about it, the more I cross off. You?'

'I don't know. Perhaps Hessenbirger will spark something.'

'Be the least he could do.'

Gallard smiled one-sidedly into the phone. 'We mustn't knock him, Elmo. You and I are of interest. He ranks with Prometheus.'

'Yeah, well, no wonder they staked him out for the vultures.'

The conversation dragged to a close. Gallard put the phone down and smiled at Elizabeth, who had finished unpacking her bag and was sitting on the other single bed looking at him closely. 'I'm all right,' he said. 'For a lonely old man who has to get up too early in the morning.'

'I don't like you getting this tired,' she said.

'Well, that comes with the territory. You can give me one of those vitamin shots in the morning. That's a nice high.'

'I'm not crazy about handing those out instead of sleep.'

'Sleep is the enemy, Elizabeth. Sleep is the thief in the night,' he said, unbuttoning his shirt, fumbling at his cuff-links with his numb fingertips. 'Good night.'

'Good night, Mr Gallard.'

He turned off the light and they finished undressing in the dark, getting into their beds. He lay on his back staring up through closed lids, thinking to himself as if speaking to his wife. There had been several times when he had almost left her, because of situations not quite like this, before she died. Wherever you are, he said to himself, you've got to be laughing like hell. If you can see me. If you care. If you cared.

He lay awake for a while longer, and then finally drifted off. Then in the morning, at six, their baggage came, with United stickers over the original Eastern tags, and there was an entire set piece with Elizabeth stepping into the next room through the connecting door, and two sets of tips for the bellboy, and clutchings of blankets around shoulders, and all that fumbling and thumping, so that he was cranky and off-stride for half an hour afterwards even though the bellboy obviously thought himself no fool and added another negligible jot to Gallard's reputation which, God knew, Gallard would have liked to spare him.

5

The Churchville Engineering and Research Division of A W C Electronics Incorporated was housed in a 1960-modern building of glassed curtain-walls set in a park-like five acres off U.S. 30 Bypass. The fountain at the front was lighted pink by night. In the early glare of morning, it plumed southwestward in the wind. As Mangrum silently held the car door for Gallard and Elizabeth, an airport taxi pulled up with

Treville in it. They shook hands and exchanged good mornings all around. Mangrum led them inside.

'You boys have a good talk last night?' Treville asked when they had reached Mangrum's office and settled themselves.

'Very satisfactory,' Gallard said, waving off a tray with cups and a Thermos jug of coffee proffered by Mangrum's secretary. She looked and dressed like the hostess at a hotel dining-room. He presumed this augured for reliability. She put sugar and powdered creamer in Mangrum's cup for him, and he drank from it without wasting a premonitory sip. One might assume, Gallard decided, that there was mutual confidence between them. She looked aggressively at Elizabeth's knees. Elizabeth smiled and turned in her chair to create a somewhat more modest line of sight to her skirt hem from Mangrum. Gallard cleared his throat softly.

'How do you want to do this?' Mangrum asked, looking exactly between Gallard and Treville. 'I have everybody waiting for whenever you're ready.'

'All in one room?'

Mangrum shook his head. 'No. I have the engineers separrate. And Hessenbirger's by himself in the conference room, getting his presentation ready. One of my assistants is helping him with his charts and drawings.'

'Fine,' Gallard said. 'Leave things that way for the moment. We have some underbrush to clear out first. I'd like to see the personnel files on the other two.'

Mangrum handed them over from his desk, where they'd been lying ready. Gallard took them with a nod of appreciation. 'By the way, do all those people have coffee?' he remarked, and the secretary left the room on Mangrum's glance. Gallard worked quickly through the two folders.

The draughtsman was Knud Pogrobius, graduate of a technical academy in Sweden. He'd originally entered the USA as a member of an amateur bicycle racing team sponsored by Huskvarna. He was in his thirties and had been with AWC three years; no previous U.S. employment. Not a citizen, so not cleared for defence contract work. He'd had the usual merit raises, no promotions, and an unvaried series of *satisfactory*'s on his annual review report forms. 'Laconic,' Gallard remarked.

Mangrum said: 'Excuse me?'

'Your draughting department supervisor seems to use few words. Do you know anything about Pogrobius?'

Mangrum shook his head.

Treville said: 'You know we have a lot of draughtsmen.'

'I can understand that. What do you know about this man Hazen?' He looked at Mangrum.

'The draughting supervisor? Top-notch. Gets out a lot of work, gets it out clean, never makes special demands on the division.'

'Strengths and weaknesses?'

'Well, those are his strengths,' Mangrum said. 'I guess if he's got a weakness, it's that he's a little too fussy on government projects. Nothing wasteful – he just takes longer. Sometimes he calls things back and has them redone.'

'Never happens on house projects?'

Mangrum pondered. 'No. Not for some time.'

'How many years?'

Mangrum pursed his lips thoughtfully. 'Oh, about three.'

'Explanation?'

Mangrum shrugged. 'I'd say it might be because he knows he does a good job. He's just a little more self-critical on contract work.' He had brought the words out slowly, and he was frowning over a new thought.

Gallard smiled at him. 'Pogrobius works only on house projects. He joined us three years ago.'

'I noted that from his file.'

'He's making his supervisor look good.'

Mangrum nodded. 'I've been thinking that.'

Treville said: 'It's to a supervisor's credit if he can find and keep good people.'

'Yes. Who hired Hazen?' he asked offhandedly.

'I did,' Mangrum said.

'Well, that's to your credit,' Gallard replied mildly. 'All right now, let's see about this girl.' He tapped his fingertips busily against the back of the other Manila folder. 'Grace Chute. Grace Chute, Class of '69 Churchville South High School, diploma in Business Arts, white female American age nineteen, marital status single, value to AWC marginal. Job performance passable, absenteeism just within acceptable limits, wages commensurate with value. The purpose of this horse is to occupy the space that would otherwise be filled by another horse.' He looked up at Mangrum. 'What's your impression of her?'

Mangrum shrugged.

'Well, suppose your son announced their engagement?' Gallard studied the manager's face. 'I see. Do you have a son?'

'I have a daughter. In college.' His eyes flickered sidewards to a corner of his desk, where a small leather-backed photo easel stood alone. Apparently he did not keep a picture of his wife in his office.

'I'm sure she makes you proud,' Gallard said sincerely. He thought of his own one child disappeared into the maw of Haight-Ashbury and was glad again that his wife was dead. 'Well, all right. I think we have a working fix on this situation.' He closed both folders and laid them on Mangrum's desk.

Mangrum said: 'Hessenbirger couldn't have done more damage if he'd picked them out deliberately.'

'Quite so.' Gallard smiled down at the floor. He scratched

absently behind his right ear, then stretched out in his chair and folded his hands in his lap. 'I had a friend in college who had no head for betting. It infuriated good players to be in poker games with him. It frustrated them to see him winning less money than they might have.'

Treville said: 'This draughtsman has no handles on him. He could leave us any time and get a job with somebody else.'

'Yes,' Gallard agreed. 'He has a skilled speciality, no particular career, no family, no responsibilities.'

'And this underage girl is dynamite.'

'Doesn't even know what's happening,' Mangrum said. 'There's no telling what she'll do.'

'Ah, well,' Gallard said, 'she and Pogrobius have had quite some time to sit and think. They'll each have pared down to a few options. They'll be nowhere near as pliable as they might have been.'

Mangrum said: 'I don't see what else I could have done with them. If I'd turned them loose –'

Gallard doubted if Hessenbirger would have let that happen. But that was beside the present point. 'You did exactly the right thing, Harry,' he said. 'Your instincts were perfect.'

'I don't know about that,' Treville demurred. 'They're going to be pretty hard to get along with.'

Gallard smiled at him kindly. Mangrum had been starting a newly relieved expression, and Treville had doused it. A salesman like Charlie ought to have weighed how many points it would cost him to assert an opinion just now. But then, Treville was under a strain. And, of course, he was a president now, and presidents run things. They don't sit back quietly in the manner of board chairmen. And it is difficult, Gallard admitted to himself, to know how to help things develop at their own pace, when there is great urgency upon one. 'We do appear to be dealing from weakness,' he said agreeably.

Mangrum, he noticed, was watching him closely. He appeared to be learning something. Gallard smiled again. 'Now, then,' he said. 'We have a great many rows to hoe this morning. Let's have the girl in here.' He nodded to Mangrum, who immediately picked up his desk phone and spoke into it. Gallard turned his countenance on Treville. 'Charles, I assume you feel we have to make the best of a bad situation with this person. It may be very difficult for all of us.'

'I don't see any other way. We've got to get things back under control.'

'It's aggravating that someone with her brains in her pants might have a multibillion-dollar entity at her mercy,' Gallard mused. 'Can you imagine what would happen if she went to the government with this story?'

'Yeah, I've thought about it,' Treville said, tight-lipped. He wiped his hand across the flesh above his mouth.

To look at him through Gallard's eyes was to share visions of plainly dressed dispassionate guerillas riddling the entire structure; of unimpressed strangers saying Yea and Nay and What's This in Charles Treville's province. Glancing at Mangrum, Gallard could see the same thing. Well, for that matter the fear and indignation were there within him, too, or he could not have detected it in these others.

'The girl's on her way up,' Mangrum said.

'Let's hope she doesn't give us too rough a time,' Gallard said.

Mangrum began: 'Maybe Miss Farrier should –'

Gallard shook his head. 'I never know when I'm going to need Miss Farrier.' He glanced at Treville. 'Just concentrate on what Grace Chute could do to us, Charles,' he said.

Treville put his hands on his thighs and stared at Gallard. 'I don't need reminding,' he said. His fingernails dragged slowly across the fabric of his trousers. Gallard saw his Adam's apple move suddenly.

'Sorry,' Gallard said mildly, smiling.

6

Mangrum's secretary brought her to the door and hesitated. 'Please join us, Mrs Buchanan,' Gallard said as he rose from his chair. 'We'll need you to take notes of our agreement with Miss Chute.' He crossed the room and held out his hand to the girl, who stood small in the doorway, looking up at him out of darting seal-coloured eyes while she held her body still.

'I'm Clinton Gallard, Miss Chute,' he said. 'The General Office has sent me down here to do the best I can.' He tentatively squeezed her cautiously offered hand. 'This is Mr Treville, the president of the company, and you know Mr Mangrum, who heads this division. And this is Miss Farrier, who flew down here from Chicago as Mr Treville and I did. Please make yourself comfortable.' He glanced at Mangrum's secretary. 'Can Mrs Buchanan bring you another cup of coffee? Have you had breakfast? I think we can get you something from the canteen.'

'That's okay,' the girl said. 'I'm all right.' Her voice was repressed – a thin, undirected presentation of a Midwest twang full of plangent nasals that came and went in Gallard's ears as she turned her head from side to side, counting all the faces.

She was a pale, thin-boned person without much in the chest; she wore a short-skirted dress that did not mould itself too candidly to her figure, and the deep, not too tight neckline showed the edges of a pale pastel bra. Her dull brown hair was streaked with touches of something that made her a parti-coloured blonde. The bright colour of her lips was uneven, and particles of it could be seen clinging to her small, crowded front teeth. Her eyes were heavily made up, and the whiteness of her throat and bare arms betrayed the intensity of the make-up on her small, sharp-featured face. Gallard presumed someone had gone to her place and brought back a change of clothing, and her cosmetics. He noticed that the polish on her nails was thick and fresh.

Nineteen, he thought. I know where they come from, but where do they go?

Well, for this one the process would be a little different. But not essentially so.

She sat down in the chair to which Gallard had escorted her. It was the one he'd been using, selected to make it easy to watch everyone in the room. He sat down awkwardly in the visitor's chair beside Mangrum's desk, holding his body very upright and keeping his feet pulled back. He let her watch Treville fidgeting and hear Mangrum's fingertips drumming softly on his desk, and then he said: 'Well, Miss Chute, I'm sure you can understand why the company wishes that the last two days had happened a little differently.'

Her eyes again reviewed all their expressions. 'Sure,' she said, her voice beginning to gain a little strength. 'It's not the kind of thing you'd want getting out.' Gallard said nothing, and she went on. 'I mean, something like this. Where you can see tomorrow's paper, and all. If everybody knows about it, then it doesn't do you any good.' Her hands closed tightly over the flap of her vinyl purse.

'What do you suppose would happen?' Gallard asked. 'If it got out.'

'Well, the government wouldn't let you buy any stock, I guess.' She grinned. 'Bookies wouldn't even talk to you.' She glanced around.

Gallard chuckled. 'I don't suppose they would.' Treville was looking at her sourly. Mangrum, Gallard noted, was keeping a totally neutral expression, but watching him as much as her. 'No, Mrs Buchanan,' Gallard said quickly to the secretary, 'don't take this part down.' The secretary was seated on a little stepstool beside a wall of print racks. She hadn't yet touched her pencil to her book, and sent Gallard a sharp look which he overrode with: 'There's no need to write down these negotiations.'

'And people would follow your investments,' the girl said definitely.

Treville demanded: 'What do you mean by that?'

Her first smile appeared. She sat up straighter, and she looked directly into Treville's eyes. It was not something he had expected, and he blinked.

'Every time you wanted to buy a piece of property,' she said, 'you'd have to hide who you were, or everybody would make you pay a lot. I think that's what I'd do. And even if you didn't have to pay too much, your competition would build up right with you the minute they knew what you were doing. It would all cost you a lot more than it should. You'd be harassed all the time. It's like if somebody down where I live, in that part of town, you know, bought a Corvette. You'd be all the time listening for the burglar alarm, and you wouldn't get your pleasure from it.' She looked around again, but not in search of smiles. She was sitting back a little and keeping her neck straight.

'Well, now, Miss Chute,' Gallard said kindly, 'suppose we simply mass-produced this device and sold it to anyone. Then everyone would be even. Don't you think this company could do rather well from that position?'

She stared at him in dismay. 'Oh, you wouldn't do that! You wouldn't be even –' She frowned, groping for aptness. 'I mean, I thought about that part of it . . .' She brightened.

'Sure, you'd be even. But the whole world would be odd. I mean – I can't even *imagine* what it would be like, but money wouldn't be worth *anything*, and . . . and, gee, suppose you were a basketball team and you saw in the paper that you lost, well, you wouldn't even play, would you? What would that do? What would happen when it was time to print tomorrow's paper?' Her eyes grew very wide. 'I just thought of that part,' she said softly.

'Money wouldn't be worth anything,' Gallard said.

'So you're not going to sell it to anybody, are you?' she asked. 'No, you're not. I've been doing a lot of thinking, but so have you and there's more of you.' She looked around the room. 'You've got a big headache if people just know you have it.'

'Even if we kept our Corvette locked in the garage and never drove it anywhere,' Gallard agreed. He leaned forward, 'just as soon as word got around the neighbourhood.'

'What are we gonna do?' the girl asked.

Gallard smiled warmly.

'I mean it,' the girl said. 'What are we gonna do about me? Look at him –' She jerked her hard, pointed chin at Treville. 'If looks could kill, like they say. And Mr Mangrum wishes I would just dry up and go away. And Mrs Buchanan –' An expression from her small girlhood crossed her face. ' – Just can't stand it because I might get Mr Mangrum in trouble.' She took a deep breath and her eyes narrowed. She gripped her purse and plunged ahead. 'I was down on Lake Wauwasee one time last summer, you know? They have this Toad Tavern there that everybody takes his boat to and buys beer. And this boy I was with was taking me over there, and in the channel there's this other boat coming the other way right next to us. And you know who I saw sitting and drinking with each other on that other boat?' She stared from Mangrum to his secretary. 'And I never said a word to anybody. Because it's live and let live in this world. I mean, life's too short.' She looked at Treville. 'So give me a little credit, somebody.'

Gallarda began to laugh. He shook his head, his face colouring, and had difficulty keeping himself from being overwhelmed. He raised a hand. 'Grace – Really, I'm not laughing *at* you. Grace – nevertheless I'm going to make you an offer.'

She was blushing and keeping her eyes away from Mangrum and his secretary. 'Okay,' she said softly.

'Mrs Buchanan, please take this down. Miss Chute, you're in a unique position regarding certain technical developments at this division of AWC Electronics Incorporated. Call it "the company". Although you don't have the technical training to understand the principles and applications involved, you've demonstrated an ability to speculate on the social consequences of a device or devices stemming from these developments and all related research. Although you recognize that those devices are proprietary to the company, you have retained your right to free speculation on their theoretical effects in the market-place. Would you allow me to describe it that way?'

'I think it makes sense.'

'Thank you. Now – did you have time to do any of this kind of talking with anyone before you were asked to come up to Mr Mangrum's office the other day?'

'Well, gee, no – I mean, Doctor Hessenbirger gave me this dime. He was laughing and joking, the way he does.' She smiled. 'He's nice. I mean, he likes to come up behind you and blow in your ear, but it's just how he says "Glad to see you", you know? Anyway, he gave it to me and said to show it around to the other girls and see what they made of it. Just for something to break up the day. I didn't know there was any big deal about it until Mrs Buchanan came downstairs and hustled me out of there just like that. And then of course when we were all sitting here and Mr Mangrum began talking serious, I started keeping my ears open.' She looked at Mrs Buchanan. ' 'Cause it's not right, hustling people.'

'No.' Gallard smiled. 'I'm sure we all wish we hadn't been quite so excited. Since then, you haven't discussed this with anyone except Doctor Hessenbirger and Mr Pogrobius?'

'Well, with Knud, mostly. I haven't seen much of Doctor Hessenbirger.'

'Some of us,' Mrs Buchanan said distinctly, 'have seen too much of him.'

Gallard sighed. 'And some of us are too old to have seen everything. Let us resume. Miss Chute, it appears that in keeping with your position as an AWC employee in good standing, you have not offered your speculations to anyone outside the company, or anyone within the company who did not already know about these developments. Make that "these subject developments", Mrs Buchanan. Therefore, you are in effect offering us your services as a marketing applications consultant. And as a duly authorized management representative of the company, I'm prepared to offer you certain terms of employment in that capacity. Clear so far, Grace?'

The girl cocked her head to one side. Gallard wondered if she had once sat that same way in her parents' parlour, listening to remonstrances with her hands stiff and her eyes searching, but her feet planted flat on the floor, and had got up at the end and moved out nevertheless. 'I think I see what we're getting to,' she said. 'Go ahead.'

'We're offering you a base annual salary of twelve thousand dollars,' Gallard said, and paused to give her an eyeblink's time before he went on. 'And a fringe benefit programme of investments, plus the usual executive insurance benefits. The investment programme is an incentive, to be funded on a one-for-one basis with your salary. The salary, of course, will rise on the normal executive review schedule.

'What it boils down to, Grace, is that if AWC's profits continue to rise, we can presume you've made a contribution to that. So for every dollar you draw in gross pay, a matching dollar will be invested for you, fifty cents in AWC stock and fifty cents in the same securities that appear in AWC's own corporate holdings portfolio. In effect, our chairman and board of directors would be your investment counsellors. And our Comptroller's Division will help you with your tax returns, if you'd like. It will all grow into quite a good thing, the longer it runs.'

The girl considered it with private little flickers of expression. 'I don't know,' she said thoughtfully. 'We'd never get away with it around here.'

Gallard grinned at her. 'Grace, if I were thirty, I'd court you. We're going to send you to San Francisco, if that's all right.'

'San Francisco?'

'The microwave plant; that's kind of half manufacturing and half engineering. There's a young fellow named Bob Cadwallader running things out there. You'd be reporting directly to him. I believe he has a thirty-six-foot sailboat and drinks Olympia. Some people say it's better than Coors.' He turned his expression directly into Treville's face, ignoring the suddenly dilated pupils he found there. 'I wonder if that's what Elmo Daugherty meant when he admitted being over a barrel. Charles, all these arrangements are agreeable to you, aren't they? Good, Mr Mangrum, do you concur in Miss Chute's transfer? Fine – now, Grace, what do you say?'

She grinned at him. 'Mr Gallard, how did you ever get euchred out of being president? You got me.' She was breathless but she was holding on. 'How's – how's fifteen thousand, and everything else matches?'

Gallard turned to Mangrum. 'You see, Harry? That's what they learn in the corridors, between classes. That's to teach us to respect her. Fifteen thousand it is, Grace, and we'll pay your moving expenses.'

'Okay.' She was suddenly on the verge of giggling. She stood up imitating a businesslike demeanour. 'Is Doctor Hessenbirger going to be in trouble? Or Knud?'

'No,' Gallard said.

'We all been waiting for Doctor Hessenbirger to get let go. With all the cutting down that's been happening with the junior technicians and all.'

'He won't be let go, Grace. Nor Mr Pogrobius. Their careers are safe.' He ignored Mangrum and Treville.

'Well, that's good, that's okay, then,' she said. But he had seen her relinquishing that surface concern from the moment he had begun reassuring her. She was nineteen, and she had sailboats in her eyes ... in time they, too, would be superseded.

'Mrs Buchanan,' he said, turning, 'if you please, type that up right away, with places for Mr Treville's signature and mine as well as Miss Chute's. Copies for everybody, copy to Cadwallader, copy to Mr Daugherty. All confidential. You and Mr Mangrum can sign as witnesses.'

Holding herself very stiffly the secretary left the room. Then they sat working out the last details – where she would stay meanwhile, when she would leave; she would take care of what she'd say to her parents – it was not a matter of moment – and so, bit by bit, it was all taken care of. Mrs Buchanan returned with the typed agreement; he proofread it, and they all signed. Mrs Buchanan left for her desk beside the door. Grace put her copy carefully in her purse. 'Well, goodbye,' she said, and they all shook hands. She went out of the door and walked away down the corridor, another historical personage.

Treville, Mangrum and Gallard sat looking at each other. Gallard was damned if he was going to speak first; there was too much hanging in the air. Mangrum was looking down at his desktop with a crooked, thin smile. Finally, he looked up and said: 'Cheap at twice the price.'

Gallard shook his head. It was all right for now, and after he'd called Cadwallader and explained the situation to him, she'd be under the eye of a man with his brains about him. But she would inch it up. She was moving forward hesitantly now, but nevertheless her pace was sixty seconds per minute, and she would not be the same any longer than that permitted. The processes would take hold; the appetites would grow as the boredom set in. And the intake would determine the shape of the organism. He would not like to see her again.

Treville could understand that as well as anyone could. But that was not what made him so snappish when he said: 'Mr Gallard never works cheap.'

7

'Well, however that may be,' Gallard said with a pleasant smile, 'let's now go discover how Pogrobius has decided to play his stake. We'll go to him. Different strokes for different folks. Lead the way, please, Harry.'

In the corridor, he took occasion to draw Mangrum aside briefly. 'No sweat, Harry,' he said softly. 'But don't bring her with you when you move up to the General Office. Country gentlewomen discover charge accounts in the big city.' He pressed lightly on Mangram's shoulder, urging him back into the lead, and the little group made its way into the room where the draughtsman was waiting.

Pogrobius had a broad, open face and massive, nearly hairless forearms protruding from his rolled-up white sleeves.

He was sitting still behind a steel table, his necktie open and his suitcoat hanging over the back of the chair. He had a scratch pad on which he'd been doodling – old-fashioned flying machines, Gallard noticed, full of wings and wires. His eyes were tigerish green above his flat cheeks, their colour undimmed by his short, straw-coloured lashes.

Mangrum nodded to the junior manager type in the room. 'All right, Jim,' he said, 'you can go get on that Matsushita proposal now,' and the assistant left. Pogrobius stood up. He was the chunky, dense-bodied type, Gallard saw; there was a touch of Finn in his ancestery, and Finns are warlocks.

'Good morning,' Gallard said. 'I'm Clinton Gallard; you know who I am.'

Progrobius thrust out his hand. 'Yes. Good morning to you.' He had an abrupt way with the language. They shook hands, and Pogrobius waited again.

Gallard said: 'I know what I'd want if I were you.'

Pogrobius showed white, square teeth. 'You have made Grace temporarily rich, correct? Would you like to try making me rich?'

Gallard shook his head.

'Will you assure me of no harm to Eduard Hessenbirger?'

'Certainly. But that's not a term.'

'No, that confirms a foregone conclusion.' Pogrobious repeated the quick huntsman's smile, this time adding a nod. 'You know, he is a remarkable man.'

Gallard said: 'Yes, he is. Tell me – do we have to all sit down in this windowless compartment and negotiate, or can we reach a quick agreement and let you get back on the job?'

'Well, go ahead with your agreement.'

'All right.' Gallard held up his left hand and began ticking off its fingers. 'First, we get a Senator to sponsor a private bill making you a citizen right away. Second, an employment contract. Third, the contract is for Assistant Supervisor of Draughting, if that's what you want; something else you're qualified for if it's not.'

'No, draughting is all right. I'm not educated in engineering.'

'Very well. Fourth, when the bill comes through, a promotion to Supervisor. Fifth, that's contingent.'

Pogrobius raised his eyebrows. His face took on a look of innocence. 'Contingent on what?'

'On whether you prove to be a good assistant supervisor in Mr Mangrum's judgement, and then as soon as he finds another honourable slot for Hazen.'

'Ah. That's wise,' Pogrobius said. 'And you give me all this because I am the best draughtsman in the division, because when you look at me it's obvious I would be a good boss.'

'We're giving it to you now for obvious reasons,' Gallard said. 'I would also like to add my apologies as company representative; you should have had a chance at it sooner.'

Pogrobius ran his tongue between his lip and his lower teeth. 'It's good to be a friend of Eduard's.'

'It's not bad to be a graduate of the Gotteborg Technical Gymnasium,' Gallard said in halting Swedish. 'Or to know what it is to be a team racer.' In English, he said with a wink : 'Don't sell America short.' He shook Pogrobius's hand again. 'We have an agreement, then.'

'Yes,' Progrobius said.

'Excellent. I'm pleased with myself. Harry – you'll get the contract ready today, right? Put a rider on it about the citizenship thing. It'll fit, because we're picking up the tab as a contract benefit. Another thing – Mr Pogrobius is fully entitled to suitable greater responsibilities as they come up over the years; I'm sure he'll be expecting normal consideration on his merits. Put a note in his personal file. If he gets shafted, I'll come back and haunt this place.' He did not smile. Neither did he frown.

Mangrum nodded. 'Yes, sir.'

'Mr Pogrobius, it was pleasant meeting you.'

Pogrobius nodded. 'The same for me. Eduard speaks well of you.'

'Well, we understand each other.'

'He said there would be very little bullshit after you arrived.'

'That remains to be seen,' Gallard said. 'Good morning.'

'You will straighten things out for him, next?' Gallard turned back from the doorway. 'I'm here to straighten out things for the company.'

Pogrobius blanked. Then he said: 'Ah, well, it may be the same thing.'

They filed out. Mangrum had offered his hand to Pogrobius and the draughtsman had taken it after a steady-eyed pause. In the hallway, Gallard said: 'Thank you, Harry. Some people don't know when to stop managing. But you gave those two enough time to decide what their positions were going to be, and then it was easy to tip them our way. I hate moving targets.'

Mangrum shrugged. 'Didn't do it deliberately.'

'Perhaps not. But it appears you have a useful style. Style counts. Details follow.' Gallard smiled, then so did Mangrum.

They proceeded along the hallway for a while. Treville was thin-lipped. Suddenly he put on a mock jovial air and punched Mangrum lightly on the shoulder. 'Never figured you'd let somebody else shuffle one of your departments, Harry,' he chuckled.

Mangrum showed puzzlement. 'Mr Gallard has the right answers,' he said. 'And Pogrobius deserved it. I don't mind at all.'

Treville turned on Gallard. He spread his arms broadly. 'What am I going to do with this man, Clint? You've conned him and he doesn't even know it.' He turned back to Mangrum. His grin was white at the corners, and his eyes were slitted. 'If you'd had more chances to watch him operate when *he* was president, you'd be a harder sell.'

Mangrum said slowly: 'I suppose that could be.' He shifted his glance towards Gallard. 'What's our next move, Mr Gallard?'

Gallard's eyes crinkled. 'Well, you'd probably want to get with your engineers now. They'll want to know there's going to be an important research role for them in the coming years. And then you'll want to prime up a little for Hessenbirger's presentation. I'm going to need a little time alone with him first. So why don't you and the engineers meet us in the conference room in twenty minutes.'

Mangrum nodded. 'Yes, sir. Excuse me, Mr Treville, Miss Farrier.' He turned and walked away.

'Charles,' Gallard remarked, 'people need to feel they've cooperated in events.'

Treville said huskily, 'What do you mean by that?'

'You're hurting yourself.'

'How?'

'You see me moving Cadwallader into position. You see me shifting Mangrum towards thinking more about managing and less about who had what prerogatives, and you're fighting it. After you retire, you'll be bitter because you fought and lost. Ease off, Charles. I told you I wasn't coming back. I'll be gone soon, and you can be president again. You'll have a few years, and you can enjoy them.' Gallard's eyes were steady. He held up his hand. 'Please just listen for a moment.

'Charles, in a year or two, Mangrum has to move into the General Office. He'll be thinking he's being held back. And he'll be realizing he doesn't have anything to hold him here, with his daughter graduated out of his house forever. There's only one reason why men his age fall in love with their secretaries. It's the shortest step towards one last time of being able to drink and laugh aboard a pleasure craft on a soft summer night. But that palls; it's a lot of trouble to arrange, and it takes up space in the managerial capacities of the brain. He'll have come to feel that way. But you don't have to care about any of that; you'll just want him where you can keep a closer eye on him. And then Cadwallader moves here, because he's in the know and because he's the best engineering manager we have. Grace will be an enormously demanding and self-indulgent problem by then. But good management will have mitigated things as much as possible. Everything will be proceeding handily. And you can be the good shepherd.'

Treville bit his lip. He stepped forward. But then he spared one look sidewards.

Gallard smiled. 'Don't consider Miss Farrier a witness. She is solely my problem.'

Treville said: 'I can take apart anything you can build.'

Gallard shook his head. 'Oh, no. Then you'd need me back to put it together again. And I won't be here. I'll be where no cool breezes can reach me.'

Treville opened his mouth. Then one could see him remembering with what feelings he had called Elmo Daugherty yesterday, and, looking at him with interest, Gallard could see the doom mirrored in his eyes.

'All right,' Treville said. 'Now you've told me.'

'I wouldn't con you, Charles,' Gallard said. 'I wouldn't make it that easy for you, you son of a bitch.'

And now you see it plainly, Gallard thought to himself, still smiling. You see it as a perfectly understandable case of revenge, and when they hand you the gold watch in a few years, that's the package you can carry it away in. 'Come along, Elizabeth,' he said. 'Mr Treville probably wants to try making a phone call before he joins us downstairs.'

They walked away. After they had turned a corner, Gallard stopped beside a water fountain and rested one shoulder lightly against the wall. 'My vision is going grey at the edges,' he said, 'and I'm getting a slight irregularity.'

She put her middle finger against the inside of his wrist and reached into her bag with the other hand. He smiled down at her with a softening of his lips, and reached out to lightly touch her hair.

'Push your sleeve up,' she said.

When they were done together, they took the elevator one flight down and walked to the conference room. Another of Mangrum's assistants was waiting outside the doors. Mangrum had called ahead and told him Gallard was coming, so the man was not surprised. He eyed calmly along Elizabeth's body until he noticed that she was rubbing the sides of her fingertips against the wet skin of her cheekbones; then he was embarrassed.

'Would you please go and unlock Doctor Hessenbirger's laboratory,' Gallard said to him. 'I'll be looking in on it before the presentation.' The assistant hurried away. Gallard pushed on the conference room doors.

8

The conference room bulletin boards were spotted with exhibits and pieces of yellow legal pad paper with red felt-tip writing. Eduard Hessenbirger, wearing a long white cotton coat open over his tweed suit, sprawled in a chair he had pulled back from one end of the long table so he could throw a leg over one of its arms. He waved negligently. 'Hello,

Clint.' He studied Elizabeth, frowned momentarily, seemed to search his mind, shrugged, and resumed smiling.

He was a long-jawed red-haired man in his forties, with knobby fingers and prominent teeth. The top of his scalp was bare; the hair at the sides was beginning to mix with white and was worn carelessly, so that pink wisps hung over the tips of his ears. There was hardly a line on his face, unless one stood very close to him. A pair of glasses with yellowing clear plastic frames rested on the bridge of his bony nose, their temples askew.

'Hello, Eduard,' Gallard said absently, walking along the walls and studying the exhibits. 'This is Miss Farrier. Elizabeth, Doctor Hessenbirger.' He paused in front of a pinned-up first page of the Red Flash edition of the *Chicago Daily News* for 8 April, 1975. He studied it for a long time and turned away. 'God *is* dead,' he said, 'and Mickey Spillane has the position.' He made his way back to where Elizabeth sat with Hessenbirger frowning at her.

'You can't see it when you're walking around in it,' Hessenbirger said.

'No, I don't suppose you can,' Gallard remarked as he took the chair next to Elizabeth. He glanced around the room. 'Why all this stuff on the bulletin boards?'

'Ah, well, you said a presentation. So we give them the whole thing, right? The lab smock, the show and tell – after all, it's like a New Product Committee meeting, isn't it?' Hessenbirger's eyes sparkled. He looked at Gallard conspiratorially. 'The 1971 model Telechron from AWC. So, we can't call it that, but I'm sure Marketing will come up with something snappy. Meanwhile, the bean-counters from Accounting will want to know how much, so that's all over there by the fire extinguisher; all costs to date, with overhead figured in as a separate item – and Manufacturing will want to know what sort of tooling might be involved, so that's right there above the wastebasket, because it's all nonsense, of course. By the light switches is where Legal will find references to prior art, which is a note from me saying I don't think Herbert George Wells is in a position to sue. Sales will want to know about cabinetwork, and that's the Polaroid you see over behind the slide projector stand. And then of course there is a list of all the strong sales features – I'm particularly proud of the fact that it can easily be all-transistorized and microlithic; solid-state, we can tell the poor boobs in their little tract houses. For O.E.M., I suggest the medical supply market – no psychiatrist's office should be complete without a machine that lets you see yourself as others see you; we sell the hardware, the O.E.M. customer builds the cabinet complete with couch and security blanket, choice of pink or blue, and padded restraining straps, of course – and I also think this can be sold in kit form for the do-it-yourself people. Some of the components are presently worth hundreds of hours of handwork each, and in order to understand the directions you must discard the notion that electrons are particles in motion, when they are in fact static filaments through which time is combed, but with modern space-age technology, what sort of obstacle is that?' Hessenbirger waved his arm again, and giggled.

'What good is it?'

'Good? My friend, it takes you four years forward into the future, almost to the day. No farther. Is this somehow related to the need for leap years? Good? Of what use, sir, is a newborn baby? Of course, every material application involves violations of postdated copyrights and patents, to say nothing of outright theft. But if we let it get out, perhaps all such conventions will be meaningless. We can throw out everything after Genesis and write a new set of instructions. Services – yes, perhaps it will be possible to set up service organizations which will turn a nice buck, but first I suggest we determine whether the future is as linear as the past, or whether it is multiplex, contrary to what the past appears to be. I have not run tests on what happens when you do something to contradict tomorrow's newspaper, nor am I anxious to persuade my grandson to shoot me. Good? I will underscore the obvious – the good of this device to AWC is that it has saved my job, probably gotten Knud into a better position *vis-à-vis* that bumbler Hazen, and made such a mess that they had to bring you back to keep this corporation the way it should be.' Hessenbirger stood up and bowed. 'I take full credit.'

'Has it occurred to you that I might not have wanted to come back?'

Hessenbirger looked at him owl-eyed. 'Well, my friend, you know you don't turn these things on and off like a water spigot. First you have it occur to you that a thing can be done, and then, late at night when you've become very bored with cutting and pasting the apparatus, you divert yourself by thinking what can be done with it. And then things proceed – one does not deny an idea. Otherwise, the brain gets constipated, right? And of course one thinks of the incredible stupidity of men like Treville and his cronies, and one does not hold back one's hand.'

'No, I don't suppose one does,' Gallard admitted. He smiled, and shook his head.

Hessenbirger had once again found a vacant space within him from which to pause and study Elizabeth. 'I know you,' he said slowly. 'No – wait – pictures. Yes. Newspaper halftones. Farrier. Let me see – you were wearing a light coat coming down some courthouse steps, so it was either spring or autumn . . .'

Elizabeth raised her eyes.

Hessenbirger snapped his fingers. 'Doctor Elizabeth Farrier. The clinic. Of course. Late last year.' He smiled suddenly and began moving towards her, putting out his hand. 'I am delighted to meet you. Truly. It is a pleasure to meet someone who fights the system. God-damned barbarians. Some of us must teach them it's not all their way. They would rather fill their slums with potential voters than do something for people. The incredible stupidity of taking away a physician's licence and throwing her in jail –'

'Putting me on probation,' Elizabeth said.

'Whatever. When all you were trying to do was help those girls.'

'I was an abortionist,' Elizabeth said as she shook his hand. 'That was what I was, and that's probably what I will be again someday. Pleased to meet you, Doctor Hessenbirger.' She sat back down again without having smiled. Hessenbirger looked at her awkwardly.

'We don't have a great deal of time,' Gallard said. 'And I want to see your machine before the engineers arrive. Can we visit your laboratory for a moment, Ed?'

'Oh, sure. Come on. Let's go.'

The three of them went down along the corridors leading towards the back of the building. Gallard said: 'How does it work, Ed?'

'Oh, that. Well, it's rather interesting. First of all, it moves only into the future; I have no method for reaching the past, although I've thought about it some and made a few attempts. I suspect the past is linear. Putting it another way, I can't comb back against the nap. That may not be quite the same thing.

'Then, there is some sort of drag. I think there may be conservation of entropy. But it takes twenty minutes objective time to get back from the four year limit, and from beyond four years, nothing gets back at all. I made some animal experiments and so forth. I suspect we will need some sort of amplifier to travel farther; I think what happens is that we are on a sort of teeter-totter, in which the forward trip, down the entropy gradient, puts sufficient energy into the system to allow a slower rebound to the starting point, but then returns diminish exponentially. I think things fall short – perhaps they return to the coordinates of this point in space, but at the wrong time. Of course, this thing might thus become an interstellar-travelling vehicle, but we are quite some time away from making an application of that, I think.'

Gallard shook his head. 'What can I say? You're a very important man.'

'No more or less than I was a few years ago.' Hessenbirger grinned. 'Of course, I have never sold myself short.'

'What's it like? How did you get the newspapers and things?'

Walking along beside Gallard, Hessenbirger shrugged. 'Nothing to it. I arrive, so to speak, in the laboratory. The machine is there; I leave the lab, go to the reception area, use the pay phone to call a cab, and I go downtown to the big newsstand. I pay for everything with the perfectly legal money in my pocket, and they give me change. I take the cab back, I go to my laboratory, and I throw the switch the other way. It's exactly like any other trip, except that I have consumed twenty minutes of 1971 time, without respect to time spent in 1975. If I see somebody in the halls, I smile and nod and keep going. I am the eccentric Doctor Hessenbirger and no one speaks to me until spoken to.'

'You're not waiting for yourself?'

'No, and I don't think I ever will be. In my life, I've from time to time caught unwarned glimpses of myself in what I didn't know was a mirror. And every so often my acquaintances point out people they swear look and act just like me. I'm sure it happens to everyone; the world's gene pool is large but finite. I have never enjoyed it; have you?'

'I've been startled.'

'Yes, that's one way to put it. At any rate, I intend to keep careful schedules. Of course, sometimes, as a very careful experiment ... perhaps I'll become curious whether two heads are better than one. But I think I'll wait until I have something very serious to discuss. Otherwise, it's just onanism, you know? Well, here we are. Wait – I'll get the light switches ... Doctor Farrier, after you ...'

Hessenbirger's area was a large room beyond the office and work rooms used by the engineers. It was in the usual state of clutter, with all sorts of equipment Gallard did not understand, though he had the vocabulary to give perhaps accurate names to most of it. Gallard stood in the doorway, looking at the pegboard booth, into which wires led in neatly taped bundles.

Hessenbirger waved towards it.

'There it is,' he said. 'Ta-ra! Step this way, lady and gentleman ...' He walked over to the wall and pushed the three-pronged plug back into the outlet. He dusted his hands as he straightened. 'Well, that's it. Greater than fire or the wheel, but perhaps not as elegant to the eye.'

Gallard said: 'I don't understand how the power goes into the future with you.'

'Oh, it does and it doesn't. First of all, it gives me the initial surge that lets me go over the edge of the entropy gradient, so to speak. All the time I'm travelling, the system is loading with energy because I'm travelling from a universe with a higher energy level. When I arrive in 1975, the heat-death is four years closer, after all. All the machine here has to do is maintain tuning; it draws only as much power as it needs to keep itself operating – it doesn't really do any of the work. Meanwhile, I arrive in 1975 with the contents of the booth, which include the controls. The controls are synchronized to the system; when I want to return, I have access to the accumulated energy, which of course is back here in time. It can't be in 1975, because that would change the 1975 entropy level, and it would be absurd. It doesn't matter whether the machine is powered in 1975, and as a matter of fact, it isn't. I assume there's another machine somewhere that is reaching 1979, or perhaps even farther. Even if I powered up this machine in 1975, I couldn't use it to reach another four years, because the only controls belong to 1971. There can't be anything already inside the booth when I arrive, or there would be things attempting to occupy each other's space, you see? Even so, there is some body heat, and a rather dramatic puff of wind, but nothing insupportable. These are all aspects that can be explored; there is ramification enough for a dozen careers.'

'I certainly suppose so,' Gallard agreed. He glanced at his watch. 'I've put some things in motion,' he said. 'I hope Bob Cadwallader will be the manager here by 1974 at the latest. Perhaps sooner.'

Hessenbirger grinned his appreciation. 'Good! Very good!' He smiled and shook his head. 'So I did do a good job for us, then. I thought to myself that a sly old fox like you could make something useful of all this.'

Gallard smiled back. 'I do the best I can, for a man who can't foretell the future.'

'Would you like to go? It's ridiculously simple.'

'No – no, not now. We have a meeting in five minutes. Treville is trying to get Elmo Daugherty to rescind my arrangements; I have some very difficult moments ahead of me, and I want to meet them on time.'

He leaned his shoulder against the doorframe and rubbed his hand over his eyes. 'Elizabeth,' he said, 'do you have anything in that magic bag for me?'

'You're ill!' Hessenbirger said. 'I didn't know that!'

Gallard shook his head. 'I'm not ill. I'm dying. Too many things have shut off in my arteries. Even with Doctor Farrier, it's just a matter of time. But I'll be all right in a moment. I function.' He looked up and smiled at Hessenbirger. 'I do it all in increments, you see, and somehow they add up to a day or two at a time.'

Elizabeth was taking his pulse and looking searchingly into his face.

'One thing,' Gallard said over her shoulder.

'What?'

'Is the machine ready? If you could go out to the 1975 reception room, and see who's listed as manager in the inter-office phone book ...'

'Yes, I can do that,' Hessenbirger said.

'I'd appreciate it. I'll go to the conference room and fight a delaying action until you get there.'

Hessenbirger's excitement shone through his concern. 'Of course! Drama! The messenger from Marathon! It doesn't matter what you say or do, Gentlemen, the accomplished fact is as follows, Zum! We got 'em right here!' He held up his hand, palm up, fingers curled. He turned towards the machine. He laughed suddenly and stripped off the ludicrous coat tossing it aside. He busied himself in the booth.

'Mr Gallard,' Elizabeth said softly, 'you're not having an episode of any sort. There's a slight acceleration of the pulse, but –'

'Hush darling,' Gallard said.

9

Gallard and Elizabeth made their way up the hallways, ignoring the confusion in the darkened offices. The power failure was confined to this wing of the building, and in due course they reached the lights of the conference room. Looking in through the doorway, Gallard could see the four engineers and Mangrum studying the walls. Treville was waiting in the hall.

'Where's Hessenbirger?' he asked.

'He'll be along. What did Elmo tell you, Charles?'

'He'd said he'd review the situation. He wants you to call him as soon as this presentation's over.' Treville smiled tautly. 'One thing you've done for us, Clint. By cooling out Pogrobius and that Chute girl, you've given us time to think over if we meant what you said to them. And they'll be fat, dumb and happy meanwhile, because they got it straight from the great Gallard's mouth.'

'Ah. All right – let's go in.'

'How soon is Hessenbirger going to get here? Look at this crap he's got put up! What does he think this corporation is – a joke?'

'No. Neither does he consider himself fit to be taken lightly. He's no different from you or me, Charles.' He smiled in a kindly manner and pressed lightly against Treville's arm to move him into the room.

'That could be,' Treville said, 'but you've got him boxed in for us, and that's what counts. He made a big splash, but you scooped all the water back in the bucket for us. There's only him to deal with now: nobody's going to talk, nobody's going to rock any boats. If we tell him *we're* going to want things in a certain way –'

'No fear, Charles,' Gallard said. 'The next four years will

see most of your policies in full force. And after that, what do you care? You and your poor circulatory condition can retire to Arizona, and what strangers do to your company won't seem important at all.' He brushed by Treville and stepped into the room. 'Gentlemen,' he said. 'You are going to be very important to this company over the coming years. You can ignore that twaddle on the bulletin boards. Concentrate on the existing research notes and the engineering memos; and of course you can study Doctor Hessenbirger's equipment all you wish, as long as you don't disturb the arrangement of the operator's booth itself. On 8 April 1975, and then on the 10th, you will keep clear of the labs. On the 10th, at about this time, I suggest a responsible company representative be in the reception room. Perhaps he'd better be there a little ahead of time, just to be sure.'

Gallard sat down. Everyone was watching him. 'Tell Doctor Hessenbirger not to attempt to return to 1971. I pulled the plug. That backlashed a lot of energy into the system; he had shunts built into it, but it still blew all the fuses in the east wing. His power source is gone.' Gallard looked around him at the other men, his smile ending directed at Treville. 'I don't suppose it really matters if he's met in 1975 or not; he's there now, and he can't travel into the past. But it would be polite, not to say potentially useful, to be courteous to him. He'll be angry enough as it is.' He closed his eyes and rubbed the bridge of his nose. 'It's all done, Charles,' he said. 'And can't be undone. And the company has four years to think about it.'

10

Elmo Daugherty's voice on the phone had to compete with the sound of departure announcements and the shuffle of feet in the narrow concourse. Gallard leaned as far as he could into the open, three-sided booth with its symmetrically drilled metal facings. 'Well, Elmo, it's just a matter of having the better brains in the company begin working out subsidiaries and spin-off companies that will go into the new markets. You've got four years to set up the new format and in 1975 he drops right into it and it's Gung Ho for glory. You have time to set up the right kind of connexions with the government, so there won't be any problems about licensing or federal regulation or anything like that; you'll have what you want, and you can give away the rest and take credit for philanthropy.'

'I saw all that the minute I heard about what you did.'

'Yes, well, we're all businessmen, Elmo. We can see our hands in front of our faces. All you have to do is keep Hessenbirger happy – which he will be, of course, particularly if no one crosses what he thinks is right – and let him work on it. By 1980 or so, everything we touch now will be golden. And if you hurry and make it public as much before that as you can, Grace Chute won't quite be the major stockholder yet.'

'I wasn't planning to be here in 1980.'

'Neither am I, Elmo. Hold on tight. Leave memos where they can be found. Address them to trustworthy heads.'

A crackle interrupted the canned music from the speakers, and the Caribbean flight was called.

'Where are you, Clint?' Elmo asked quickly. 'I thought you'd be coming up to see me.'

'Whatever for, Elmo? You owe me one day's consultation

fee. Just deposit two hundred dollars in my bank account.' He hung up the phone, turned, and smiled at Elizabeth. He offered her his arm. They began to walk up the concourse. Gallard's footsteps were sure and regular. He looked up at nothing in particular, winked, and made a jerking motion of his free hand. He began to laugh. Elizabeth cast him an anxious glance. Gallard stopped capering and smiled at her, fondly. He was already, however, beginning to think of DC-3s, and then of tall white cruise ships, and of a narrow winding street of steps that led to the house where they played music on Victrolas with hand-joined, beautifully varnished boxes, nickelled cranks, and fluted horns like Morning Glories confused by the light from the great chandeliers and thus mistakenly uttering praise of a new day.

Croatoan

Harlan Ellison

It's almost impossible to gain a reputation as a writer in science fiction, or any other field, unless you write novels. The major sf writers have always been people like Heinlein, Clarke, Le Guin, Simack, Niven: though they've all done excellent short stories, you remember them for their novels. Even Ray Bradbury's reputation is based largely on his novel Fahrenheit 451.

Harlan Ellison is the notable exception. He has never written a major science fiction novel – he's written no novels at all for decades – yet he's won more awards than anyone else in science fiction and his short story collections sell and sell.

Why? Probably it's because Ellison realizes that the strength of the short story form is its ability to compress experience to an intensity seldom possible in novels. Here is an example: a short, jolting story of a man who ventures beneath our world and discovers much, much more than he seeks.

Beneath the city, there is yet another city; wet and dark and strange; a city of sewers and moist scuttling creatures and running rivers so desperate to be free not even Styx fits them. And in that lost city beneath the city, I found the child.

Oh my God, if I knew where to start. With the child? No, before that. With the alligators? No, earlier. With Carol?

Probably. It always started with a Carol. Or an Andrea. A Stephanie. Always someone. There is nothing cowardly about suicide; it takes determination.

'Stop it! Goddammit, just *stop* it ... I said stop ...' And I had to hit her. It wasn't that hard a crack, but she had been weaving, moving, stumbling: she went over the coffee table, all the fifty dollar gift books coming down on top of her. Wedged between the sofa and the overturned table. I kicked the table out of the way and bent to help her up, but she grabbed me by the waist and pulled me down; crying, begging me to *do* something. I held her and put my face in her hair and tried to say something right, but what could I say?

Denise and Joanna had left, taking the d & c tools with them. She had been quiet, almost as though stunned by the hammer, after they had scraped her. Quiet, stunned, dry-eyed but hollow-eyed; watching me with the polythene shopping bag. The sound of the toilet flushing had brought her running from the kitchen, where she had lain on a mattress pad. I heard her coming, screaming, and caught her just as she started through the hall to the bathroom. And hit her, without wanting to, just trying to stop her as the water sucked the polythene bag down and away.

'D-*do* somethi-ing,' she gasped, fighting for air.

I kept saying Carol, Carol, over and over, holding her, rocking back and forth, staring over her head, across the living-room to the kitchen, where the edge of the teak dining table showed through the doorway, the amber-stained mattress pad hanging half over the edge, pulled loose when Carol had come for the shopping bag.

After a few minutes, she spiralled down into dry, sand-papered sighs. I lifted her on to the sofa, and she looked up at me.

'Go after him, Gabe. Please. Please, go after him.'

'Come on, Carol, stop it. I feel lousy about it . . .'

'*Go after him, you sonofabitch!*' she screamed. Veins stood out on her temples.

'I *can't* go after him, dammit, he's in the plumbing; he's in the lousy river by now! Stop it, get off my case, let me alone!' I was screaming back at her.

She found a place where untapped tears waited, and I sat there, across from the sofa, for almost half an hour, just the one lamp casting a dull glow across the living-room, my hands clasped down between my knees, wishing she was dead, wishing I was dead, wishing everyone was dead . . . except the kid. But. He was the only one who *was* dead. Flushed. Bagged and flushed. Dead.

When she looked up at me again, a shadow cutting off the lower part of her face so the words emerged from darkness, keynoted only by the eyes, she said, 'Go find him.' I had never heard anyone sound that way, ever. Not ever. It frightened me. Riptides beneath the surface of her words created trembling images of shadow women drinking Drano, lying with their heads inside gas ovens, floating face up in thick, red bath water, their hair rippling out like jellyfish.

I knew she would do it. I couldn't support that knowledge. 'I'll try,' I said.

She watched me from the sofa as I left the apartment, and standing against the wall in the elevator, I felt her eyes on me. When I reached the street, still and cold in the pre-dawn, I thought I would walk down to the River Drive and mark time till I could return and console her with the lie that I had tried but failed.

But she was standing in the window, staring down at me.

The manhole cover was almost directly across from me, there in the middle of the silent street.

I looked from the manhole cover to the window, and back

again, and again, and again. She waited. Watching. I went to the iron cover and got down on one knee and tried to pry it up. Impossible. I bloodied my finger-tips trying, and finally stood, thinking I had satisfied her. I took one step towards the building and realized she was no longer in the window. She stood silently at the kerb, holding the long metal rod that wedged against the apartment door when the police lock was engaged.

I went to her and looked into her face. She knew what I was asking: I was asking, *isn't this enough? Haven't I done enough?*

She held out the rod. No, I hadn't done enough.

I took the heavy metal rod and levered up the manhole cover. It moved with difficulty, and I strained to pry it off the hole. When it fell, it made a clanging in the street that rose up among the apartment buildings with an alarming suddenness. I had to push it aside with both hands; and when I looked up from that circle of darkness that lay waiting, and turned to the spot where she had given me the tool, she was gone.

I looked up; she was back in the window.

The smell of the unwashed city drifted up from the manhole, chill and condemned. The tiny hairs in my nose tried to baffle it; I turned my head away.

I never wanted to be an attorney. I wanted to work on a cattle ranch. But there was family money, and the need to prove myself to shadows who had been dead and buried with their owners long since. People seldom do what they want to do; they usually do what they are *compelled* to do. Stop me before I kill again. There was no rational reason for my descending into that charnel house stink, that moist darkness. No rational reason, but Denise and Joanna from the Abortion Centre had been friends of mine for eleven years. We had been in bed together many times; long past the time I had enjoyed being in bed together with them, or they had enjoyed being in bed together with me. They knew it. I knew it. They knew I knew, and they continued to set that as one of the payments for their attendances at my Carols, my Andreas, my Stephanies. It was their way of getting even. They liked me, despite themselves, but they had to get even. Get even for their various attendances over eleven years, the first of which had been one for the other, I don't remember which. Get even for many flushings of the toilet. There was no rational reason for going down into the sewers. None.

But there were eyes on me from an apartment window.

I crouched, dropped my legs over the lip of the open manhole, sat on the street for a moment, then slipped over the edge and began to climb down.

Slipping into an open grave. The smell of the earth is there, where there is no earth. The water is evil; vital fluid that has been endlessly violated. Everything is covered with a green scum that glows faintly in the darkness. An open grave waiting patiently for the corpse of the city to fall.

I stood on the ledge above the rushing tide, seeing the sodden weight of lost and discarded life that rode the waters towards even darker depths. *My God,* I thought, *I must be out of my mind just to be here.* It had finally overtaken me; the years of casual liaisons, careless lies, the guilt I suppose I'd *always* known would mount up till it could no longer be denied. And I was down here, where I belonged.

People do what they are compelled to do.

I started walking towards the arching passageways that led down away from the steel ladder and the street opening above. Why not walk: aimless, can you perceive what I'm saying?

Once, years ago, I had an affair with my junior partner's wife. Jerry never knew about it. They're divorced now. I don't think he ever found out; she would have had to've been even crazier than I thought to tell him. Denise and Joanna had visited that time, too. I'm nothing if not potent. We flew to Kentucky together one week-end. I was preparing a brief, she met me at the terminal, we flew as husband and wife, family rate. When my work was done in Louisville, we drove out into the countryside. I minored in geology at college, before I went into law. Kentucky is rife with caves. We pulled in at a picnic grounds where some locals had advised us we could do a little spelunking, and with the minimal gear we had picked up at a sporting goods shop, we went into a fine network of chambers, descending beneath the hills and the picnic grounds. I loved the darkness, the even temperature, the smooth-surfaced rivers, the blind fish and water-insects that scurried across the wet mirror of the still pools. She had come because she was not permitted to have intercourse at the base of Father Duffy's statue on Times Square, in the main window of Bloomingdale's or on Channel 2 directly preceding The Late News. Caves were the next best thing.

For my part, the thrill of winding down deeper and deeper into the earth – even though graffiti and Dr Pepper cans all along the way reminded me this was hardly unexplored territory – offset even her sophomoric appeals to 'take her violently', there on the shell-strewn beach of a subterrannean river.

I *liked* the feel of the entire Earth over me. I was not claustrophobic, I was – in some perverse way – wonderfully free. Even soaring! Under the ground, I was soaring!

The walk deeper into the sewer system did not unsettle or distress me. I rather enjoyed being alone. The smell was terrible, but terrible in a way I had not expected.

If I had expected vomit and garbage, this was certainly not what I smelled. Instead, there was a bittersweet scent of rot – reminiscent of Florida mangrove swamps. There was a smell of cinnamon, and wallpaper paste, and charred rubber; the warm odours of rodent blood and bog gas; melted cardboard, wool, coffee grounds still aromatic, rust.

The downward channel levelled out. The ledge became a wide, flat plain as the water went down through drainage conduits, leaving only a bubbling, frothy residue to sweep away into the darkness. It barely covered the heels of my shoes. Florsheims, but they could take it. I kept moving. Then I saw the light ahead of me.

It was dim, flickering, vanished for a moment as something obscured it from my view, moving in front of it, back again, dim and orange. I moved towards the light.

It was a commune of bindle-stiffs; derelicts gathered together beneath the streets for safety and the skeleton of camaraderie. Five very old men in heavy overcoats and three even older men in cast-off Army jackets . . . but the older men were younger, they only *looked* older: a condition of the skids. They sat around a waste-barrel oil drum filled with fire. Dim, soft, withered fire that leaped and curled and threw off sparks all in slow motion. Dreamwalking fire; somnambulist fire; mesmerized fire. I saw an atrophied arm of flame like a creeper of kangeroo ivy emerge over the lip of the barrel, struggling towards the shadowed arch of the tunnel ceiling; it stretched itself thin, released a single, teardrop-shaped spark, and then fell back into the barrel without a scream.

The hunkering men watched me come towards them. One of them said something, directly into the ear of the man beside him; he moved his lips very little and never took his eyes off me. As I neared, the men stirred expectantly. One of them reached into a deep pocket of his overcoat for something bulky. I stopped and looked at them.

They looked at the heavy iron rod Carol had given me.

They wanted what I had, if they could get it.

I wasn't afraid. I was under the Earth and I was part iron

rod. They could not get what I had. They knew it. That's why there are always less killings than there might be. People *always* know.

I crossed to the other side of the channel, close to the wall. Watching them carefully. One of them, perhaps strong himself, perhaps merely stupider, stood up and, thrusting his hands deeper into his overcoat pockets, paralleled my passage down the channel away from them.

The channel continued to descend slightly, and we walked away from the oil drum and the light from the fire and the tired community of subterranean castoffs. I wondered idly when he would make his move, but I wasn't worried. He watched me, trying to see me more clearly, it seemed, as we descended deeper into the darkness. He moved up closer, but didn't cross the channel. I turned the bend first.

Waiting, I heard the sounds of rats in their nests.

He didn't come around the bend.

I found myself beside a service niche in the tunnel wall, and stepped back into it. He came around the bend, on my side of the channel. I could have stepped out as he passed my hiding place, could have clubbed him to death with the iron rod before he realized that the stalker had become the stalked.

I did nothing, stayed far back motionless in the niche and let him pass. Standing there, my back to the slimy wall, listening to the darkness around me, utter, final, even palpable. But for the tiny twittering sounds of rats, I could have been two miles down in the central chamber of some lost cavern maze.

There's no logic to why it happened. At first, Carol had been just another casual liaison, another bright mind to touch, another witty personality to enjoy, another fine and workable body to work so fine with mine. I grow bored quickly. It's not a sense of humour I seek – Lord knows every slithering, hopping, crawling member of the animal kingdom has a sense of humour – for christ sake even dogs and *cats* have a sense of humour – it's wit! Wit is the answer. Let me touch a woman with wit and I'm gone, sold on the spot, I said to her, the first time I met her, at a support luncheon for the Liberal candidate for DA, 'Do you fool around?'

'I don't fool,' she said, instantly, no time-lapse, no need for rehearsal fresh out of her mind, 'fools bore me. Are you a fool?'

I was delighted and floored at the same time. I went fumfuhfumfuh, and she didn't give me a moment. 'A simple yes or no will suffice. Answer this one: how many sides are there to a round building?'

I started to laugh. She watched me with amusement, and for the first time in my life I actually saw someone's eyes twinkle with mischief. 'I don't know,' I said, 'how many sides *are* there to a round building?'

'Two,' she answered, '*in*side and *out*side. I guess you're a fool. No, you may not take me to bed.' And she walked away.

I was undone. She couldn't have run it better if she had come back two minutes in a time machine, knowing what I'd say, and programmed me into it. And so I chased her. Up hill and down dale, all around that damned dreary luncheon, till I finally herded her into a corner – which was precisely what she'd been going for.

'As Bogart said to Mary Astor, "You're good, thweetheart, very, very good."' I said it fast for fear she'd start running me around again. She settled against the wall, a martini in her hand, and she looked up at me with that twinkling.

At first it was just casual. But she had depth, she had wiliness, she had such an air of self-possession that it was inevitable I would start phasing-out the other women, would start according her the attention she needed and wanted and without demanding . . . demanded.

I came to care.

Why didn't I take precautions? Again, there's no logic to it. I thought she was; and for a while, she was. Then she stopped. She told me she had stopped, something internal, the gynaecologist had suggested she go off the pill for a while. She suggested vasectomy to me. I chose to ignore the suggestion. But chose not to stop sleeping with her.

When I called Denise and Joanna, and told them Carol was pregnant, they sighed, and I could see them shaking their heads sadly. They said they considered me a public menace, but told me to tell her to come down to the Abortion Centre and they would put the suction pump to work. I told them, hesitantly, that it had gone too long, suction wouldn't work. Joanna simply snarled, 'You thoughtless bastard!' and hung up the extension. Denise read me the riot act for twenty minutes. She didn't suggest a vasectomy; she suggested, in graphic detail, how I might have my organ removed by a taxidermist using a cheese grater. Without benefit of anaesthesia.

But they came, with their dilation and curettage implements, and they laid her out on the teak table with a mattress under her, and then they had gone – Joanna pausing a moment at the door to advise me this was the last time, the very last time, the last time she could stomach it, that it was the last time and did I have that fixed firmly, solidly, embedded in the forefront of my brain?

And now I was here in the sewers.

I tried to remember what Carol looked like, but it wasn't an image I could fix in my mind half as solidly as I had fixed the thought that this. Was. The. Last. Time.

I stepped out of the service niche.

The young-old bindlestiff who had followed me was stand-there, silently waiting. At first I couldn't even see him – there was only the vaguest lighter shade of darkness to my left coming from around the bend and that oil drum full of fire – but I knew he was there. Even as *he* had known I was there, all the time. He didn't speak, and I didn't speak, and after a while I was able to discern his shape. Hands still deep in his pockets.

'Something?' I said, more than a little belligerently.

He didn't answer.

'Get out of my way.'

He stared at me, sorrowfully, I thought, but that had to be nonsense. I thought.

'Don't make me have to hurt you,' I said.

He stepped aside, still watching me.

I started to move past him, down the channel.

He didn't follow, but I was walking backward to keep him in sight, and he didn't take his eyes off mine.

I stopped. 'What do you want?' I asked. 'Do you need some money?'

He came towards me. Inexplicably, I wasn't afraid he would try something. He wanted to see me more clearly, closer I thought.

'You couldn't give me nothing I need.' His voice was rusted, pitted, scarred, unused, unwieldy.

'Then why are you following me?'

'Why've you come down here?'

I didn't know what to say.

'You make it bad down here, Mister. Why don't you g'wan and go back upside, leave us alone?'

'I have a right to be here.' Why had I said *that*?

'You got no right to come down here; stay back upside where you belong. All of us know you make it bad, Mister.'

He didn't want to hurt me, he just didn't want me here. Not even right for these outcasts, the lowest level to which men could sink; even here I was beneath contempt. His hands were deep in his pockets. 'Take your hands out of your pockets, slowly, I want to make sure you aren't going to hit me with something when I turn around. Because I'm going on down there, not back. Come on now, do it. Slowly. Carefully.'

He took his hands out of his pockets slowly and held them up. He had no hands. Chewed stumps, glowing faintly green like the walls where I had descended from the manhole.

I turned and went away from him.

It grew warmer, and the phosphorescent green slime on the walls gave some light. I had descended as the channel had fallen away deeper under the city. This was a land not even the noble street-workers knew, a land blasted by silence and emptiness. Stone above and below and around, it carried the river without a name into the depths, and if I could not return, I would stay here like the skids. Yet I continued walking. Sometimes I cried, but I don't know why, or for what, or for whom. Certainly not for myself.

Was there ever a man who had everything more than I had had everything? Bright words, and quick movements, soft cloth next to my skin, and places to place my love, if I had only recognized that it *was* love.

I heard a nest of rats squealing as something attacked them, and I was drawn to a side tunnel where the shining green effluvium made everything bright and dark as the view inside the machines they used to have in shoe stores. I hadn't thought of that in years. Until they found out that the X-rays could damage the feet of children, shoes stores used bulky machines one stepped up on to and into which one inserted newly shod feet. And when the button was pushed, a green X-ray light came on, showing the bones that lay beneath the flesh. Green and black. The light was green, and the bones were duty black. I hadn't thought of that in years, but the side tunnel was illuminated in just that way.

An alligator was ripping the throats of baby rats.

It had invaded the nest and was feeding mercilessly, tossing the bodies of the ripped and shredded rodents aside as it went for the defenceless smaller ones. I stood watching, sickened but fascinated. Then, when the shrieks of anguish were extinguished at last, the great saurian, direct lineal descendent of Rex, snapped them up one by one and, thrashing its tail, turned to stare at me.

He had no hands. Chewed stumps, glowing faintly green like the walls.

I moved back against the wall of the side tunnel as the alligator belly-crawled past me, dragging its leash. The thick, armoured tail brushed my ankle and I stiffened.

Its eyes glowed red as those of an Inquisition torturer.

I watched its scaled and taloned feet leave deep prints in the muck underfoot, and I followed the beast, its trail clearly marked by the impression of the leash in the mud.

Frances had a five-year-old daughter. She took the little girl for a vacation to Miami Beach one year. I flew down for a few days. We went to a Seminole village, where the old women did their sewing on Singer machines. I thought that was said. A lost heritage, perhaps; I don't know. The daughter, whose name I can't recall, wanted a baby alligator. Cute. We brought it back on the plane in a cardboard box with air holes. Less than a month later it had grown large enough to snap. Its teeth weren't that long, but it snapped. It was saying: this is what I'll be; direct lineal descendant of Rex. Frances flushed it down the toilet one night after we'd made love. The little girl was asleep in the next room. The next morning, Frances told her the alligator had run off.

The sewers of the city are infested with full-grown alligators. No amount of precaution and no forays by hunting teams with rifles or crossbows or flame throwers have been able to clear the tunnels. The sewers are still infested; workers go carefully. So did I.

The alligator moved steadily, gracefully in its slithering

passage down one tunnel and into another side passage and down always down, steadily into the depths. I followed the trail of the leash.

We came to a pool, and it slid into the water like oil, its dead-long snout above the fetid foulness, its Torquemada eyes looking towards its destination.

I thrust the iron rod down my pant leg, pulled my belt tight enough to hold it, and waded into the water. It came up to my neck, and I lay out and began dog-paddling, using the one leg that would bend. The light was very green and sharp now.

The saurian came out on the muck beach at the other side and crawled forward towards an opening in the tunnel wall. I crawled out, pulled the iron rod loose, and followed. The opening gave into darkness, but as I passed through, I trailed my hand across the wall and felt a door. I stopped, surprised, and felt in the darkness. An iron door, with an arched closure at the top and a latch. Studs, heavy and round and smelling faintly of rust, dotted the door.

I walked through . . . and stopped.

There had been something else on the door. I stepped back and ran my fingers over the open door again. I found the indentations at once and ran my finger-tips across them, trying to discern in the utter darkness what they were. Something about them . . . I traced them carefully.

They were letters. C. My fingers followed the curves. R. Cut into the iron somehow. O. What was a door doing down here? A. The cuts seemed very old, weathered, scummy. T. They were large, and very regular. O. They made no sense, no word formed that I knew. A. And I came to the end of the sequence. N.

CROATOAN. It made no sense. I stayed there a moment, trying to decide if it was a word the sanitation engineers might have used for some designation of a storage area, perhaps. Croatoan. No sense. Not Croatian, it was Croatoan. Something nibbled at the back of my memory: I *had* heard the word before, knew it from somewhere, long ago, a vapor of sound travelling back on the wind of the past. It escaped me, I had no idea what it meant.

I went through the doorway again.

Now I could not even see the trail of the leash the alligator had dragged. I kept moving, the iron rod in my hand.

I heard them coming towards me from both sides, and it was clearly alligators, many of them. From side passages. I stopped and reached out to find the wall of the channel. I couldn't find it. I turned around, hoping to get back to the door, but when I hurried back the way I thought I had come, I didn't reach the door. I just kept going. Either I had gone down a fork and not realized the channel had separated, or I had lost my sense of direction. And the slithering sounds kept coming.

Now, for the first time, I felt terror! The safe, warm, enfolding darkness of the underworld had, in an instant, merely by the addition of sounds around me, become a suffocating winding-sheet. It was as if I'd abruptly awakened in a coffin, buried six feet beneath the tightly stomped loam; that clogging terror Poe had always described so well because he had feared it himself . . . the premature burial. Caves no longer seemed comfortable.

I began to run!

I lost the rod somewhere, the iron bar that had been my weapon, my security.

I fell and slid face-first in the muck.

I scrabbled to my knees and kept going. No walls, no light, no slightest aperture or outcropping, nothing to give me a sense of being in the world, running through a limbo without beginning, without end.

Finally, exhausted, I slipped and fell and lay for a moment.

I heard slithering all around me and managed to pull myself to a sitting position. My back grazed a wall, and I fell up against it with a moan of gratitude. Something, at least; a wall against which to die.

I don't know how long I lay there, waiting for the teeth.

Then I felt something touching my hand. I recoiled with a shriek. It had been cool and dry and soft. Did I recall that snakes and other amphibians were cool and dry? Did I remember that? I was trembling.

Then I saw a light. Flickering, bobbing, going up and down just slightly, coming towards me.

And as the light grew closer and brighter, I saw there was something right beside me; the something that had touched me; it had been there for a time, watching me.

It was a child.

Naked, deathly white, with eyes great and luminous, but covered with a transparent film as milky as a membrane, small, very young, hairless, its arms shorter than they should have been, purple and crimson veins crossing its bald skull like traceries of blood on a parchment, fine even features, nostrils dilating as it breathed shallowly, ears slightly tipped as though reminiscent of an elf, barefooted but with pads on the soles, this child stared at me, looked up at me, its little tongue visible as it opened its mouth filled with tiny teeth, trying to form sounds, saying nothing, watching me, a wonder in its world, watching me with the saucer eyes of a lemur, the light behind the membrane flickering and pulsing. This child.

And the light came nearer, and the light was many lights. Torches, held aloft by the children who rode the alligators.

Beneath the city, there is yet another city; wet and dark and strange.

At the entrance to their land someone – not the children,

they couldn't have done it – long ago built a road sign. It is a rotted log on which has been placed, carved from fine cherry-wood, a book and a hand. The book is open, and the hand rests on the book, one finger touching the single word carved in the open pages. The word CROATOAN.

On 13 August, 1590, Governor John White of the Virginia colony managed to get back to the stranded settlers of the Roanoke, North Carolina, colony. They had been waiting three years for supplies, but politics, foul weather and the Spanish Armada had made it impossible. As they went ashore they saw a pillar of smoke. When they reached the site of the colony, though they found the stronghold walls still standing against possible Indian attacks, no sign of life greeted them. The Roanoke colony had vanished. Every man, woman and child, gone. Only the word CROATOAN had been left. '*One of the chiefe trees or postes at the right side of the entrance had the barke taken off, and 5. foote from the ground in fayre Capital letters was graven* CROATOAN *without any crosse or signe of distresse.*'

There was a Croatan island, but they were not there. There was a tribe of Hatteras Indians who were called Croatans, but they knew nothing of the whereabouts of the lost colony. All that remains of legend is the story of the child Virgina Dare and the mystery of what happened to the lost settlers of Roanoke.

Down here in this land beneath the city, live the children. They live easily and in strange ways. I am only now coming to know the incredible manner of their existence. How they eat, what they eat, how they manage to survive, and have managed for hundreds of years, these are all things I learn day by day, with wonder surmounting wonder.

I am the only adult here.
They have been waiting for me.
They call me father.

Doing Lennon

Gregory Benford

In the past few years Gregory Benford has quietly emerged as one of science fiction's best writers. Daytimes he works as a professor of physics at the University of California, Irvine; at night he retires to his study and dictates the first drafts of his stories into a tape recorder. In 1975 he won a Nebula Award, with Gordon Eklund, for their novelette 'If the Stars Are Gods'; and the following story is a Nebula nominee this year: a subtle, surprising story of a man working a con game on the future.

Sanity calms, but madness is more interesting.

John Russell

As the hideous cold seeps from him he feels everything becoming sharp and clear again. He decides he can do it, he can make it work. He opens his eyes.

'Hello.' His voice rasps. 'Bet you aren't expecting me. I'm John Lennon.'

'What?' the face above him says.

'You know. John Lennon. The Beatles.'

Professori Hermann – the name attached to the face which loomed over him as he drifted up, up from the Long Sleep – is vague about the precise date. It is either 2108 or 2180. Hermann makes a little joke about inversion of positional notation; it has something to do with nondenumerable set theory, which is all the rage. The ceiling glows with a smooth green phosphorescence and Fielding lies there letting them prick him with needles, unwrap his organiform nutrient webbing, poke and adjust and massage as he listens to a hollow *pock-pock-eta*. He knows this is the crucial moment, he must hit them with it now.

'I'm glad it worked,' Fielding says with a Liverpool accent. He has got it just right, the rising pitch at the end and the nasal tones.

'No doubt there is an error in our log,' Hermann says pedantically. 'You are listed as Henry Fielding.'

Fielding smiles. 'Ah, that's the ruse, you see.'

Hermann blinks owlishly. 'Deceiving Immortality Incorporated is –'

'I was fleeing political persecution, y'dig. Coming out for the workers and all. Writing songs about persecution and pollution and the working class hero. Snarky stuff. So when the jackboot skinheads came in I decided to check out.'

Fielding slips easily into the story he has memorized, all plotted and paced with major characters and minor characters and bits of incident, all of it sounding very real. He wrote it himself, he has it down. He continues talking while Hermann and some white-smocked assistants help him sit up, flex his legs, test his reflexes. Around them are vats and baths and tanks. A fog billows from a hole in the floor; a liquid nitrogen immersion bath.

Hermann listens intently to the story, nodding now and then, and summons other officials. Fielding tells his story again while the attendants work on him. He is careful to give the events in different order, with different details each time. His accent is standing up though there is mucous in his sinuses that makes the high sing-song bits hard to get out. They give him something to eat; it tastes like chicken-flavoured ice cream. After a while he sees he has them convinced.

After all, the late Twentieth was a turbulent time, crammed with gaudy events, lurid people. Fielding makes it seem reasonable that an aging rock star, seeing his public slip away and the government closing in, would corpsicle himself.

The officials nod and gesture and Fielding is wheeled out on a carry table. Immortality Incorporated is more like a church than a business. There is a ghostly hush in the hallways, the attendants are distant and reserved. Scientific servants in the temple of life.

They take him to an elaborate display, punch a button. A voice begins to drone a welcome to the year 2018 (or 2180). The voice tells him he is one of the few from his benighted age who saw the slender hope science held out to the diseased and dying. His vision has been rewarded. He has survived the unfreezing. There is some nondenominational talk about God and death and the eternal rhythm and balance of life, ending with a retouched holographic photograph of the Founding Fathers. They are a small knot of biotechnicians and engineers clustered around an immersion tank. Close-cropped hair, white shirts with ball-point pens clipped in the pockets. They wear glasses and smile weakly at the camera, as though they have just been shaken awake.

'I'm hungry,' Fielding says.

News that Lennon is revived spreads quickly. The Society for Dissipative Anachronisms holds a press conference for him. As he strides into the room Fielding clenches his fists so no one can see his hands shaking. This is the start. He has to make it here.

'How do you find the future, Mr Lennon?'

'Turn right at Greenland.' Maybe they will recognize it from A *Hard Day's Night*. This is before his name impacts fully, before many remember who John Lennon was. A fat man asks Fielding why he elected for the Long Sleep before he really needed it and Fielding says enigmatically, 'The role of boredom in human history is underrated.' This makes the evening news and the weekly topical roundup a few days later.

A fan of the twentieth century asks him about the breakup with Paul, whether Ringo's death was a suicide, what about Allan Klein, how about the missing lines from *Abbey Road?* Did he like Dylan? What does he think of the Aarons theory that the Beatles could have stopped Vietnam?

Fielding parries a few questions, answers others. He does not tell them, of course, that in the early sixties he worked in a bank and wore granny glasses. Then he became a broker with Harcum, Brandels and Son and his take in 1969 was 57,803 dollars, not counting the money siphoned off into the two concealed accounts in Switzerland. But he read *Rolling Stone* religiously, collected Beatles memorabilia, had all the albums and books and could quote any verse from any song. He saw Paul once at a distance, coming out of a recording session. And he had a friend into Buddhism, who met Harrison one week-end in Surrey. Fielding did not mention his vacation spent wandering around Liverpool, picking up the accent and visiting all the old places, the cellars where they played and the narrow dark little houses their families owned in the early days. And as the years dribbled on and Fielding's money piled up, he lived increasingly in those golden days of the sixties, imagined himself playing side man along with Paul or George or John and crooning those same notes into the microphones, practically kissing the metal. And Fielding did not speak of his dreams.

It is the antiseptic Stanley Kubrick future. They are very adept at hardware. Population is stabilized at half a billion. Everywhere there are white hard decorator chairs in vaguely Danish modern. There seems no shortage of electrical power or oil or copper or zinc. Everyone has a hobby. Entertainment is a huge enterprise, with stress on ritual violence. Fielding watches a few games of Combat Golf, takes in a public execution or two. He goes to witness an electrical man short circuit himself. The flash is visible over the curve of the Earth.

Genetic manipulants – *manips*. Hermann explains – are thin, stringy people, all lines and knobby joints where they connect directly into machine linkages. They are designed for some indecipherable purpose. Hermann, his guide, launches into an explanation but Fielding interrupts him to say, 'Do you know where I can get a guitar?'

Fielding views the era 1950-1980:

'Astrology wasn't rational, nobody really believed it, you've got to realize that. It was *boogie woogie*. On the other hand, science and rationalism were progressive jazz.'

He smiles as he says it. The 3D snout closes in. Fielding has purchased well and his plastic surgery, to lengthen the nose and give him that wry Lennonesque smirk, holds up well. Even the technicians at Immortality Incorporated missed it.

Fielding suffers odd moments of blackout. He loses the rub of rough cloth at a cuff on his shirt, the chill of air-conditioned breeze along his neck. The world dwindles away and sinks into inky black, but in a moment it is all back and he hears the distant murmur of traffic, and convulsively, by reflex, he squeezes the bulb in his hand and the orange vapour rises around him. He breathes deeply, sighs. Visions float into his mind and the sour tang of the mist reassures him.

Every age is known by its pleasures, Fielding reads from the library readout. The Twentieth introduced two: high speed and hallucinogenic drugs. Both proved dangerous in the long run, which made them even more interesting. The Twenty-first developed weightlessness, which worked out well except for the re-entry problems if one overindulged. In the Twenty-second there were aquaform and something Fielding could not pronounce or understand.

He thumbs away the readout and calls Hermann for advice.

Translation difficulties:

They give him a sort of pasty suet when he goes to the counter to get his food. He shoves it back at them.

'Gah! Don't you have a hamburger someplace?' The stunted man behind the counter flexes his arms, makes a rude sign with his four fingers and goes away. The wiry woman next to Fielding rubs her thumbnail along the hideous scar at her side and peers at him. She wears only orange shorts and boots, but he can see the concealed dagger in her armpit.

'Hamburger?' she says severely. 'That is the name of a citizen of the German city of Hamburg. Were you a cannibal then?'

Fielding does not know the proper response, which could be dangerous. When he pauses she massages her brown scar with new energy and makes a sign of sexual invitation. Fielding backs away. He is glad he did not mention french fries.

On 3D he makes a mistake about the recording date of *Sergeant Pepper's Lonely Hearts Club Band*. A ferret-eyed history student lunges in for the point but Fielding leans back casually, getting the accent just right, and says, 'I zonk my brow with heel of hand, consterned!' and the audience laughs and he is away free.

Hermann has become his friend. The library readout says this is a common phenomenon among Immortality Incorporated employees who are fascinated by the past to begin with (or otherwise would not be in the business) and anyway Hermann and Fielding are about the same age, forty-seven. Hermann is not surprised that Fielding is practising his chords and touching up his act.

'You want to get out on the road again, is that it?' Hermann says. 'You want to be getting popular.'

'It's my business.'

'But your songs, they are old.'

'Oldies but goldies,' Fielding says solemnly.

'Perhaps you are right,' Hermann sighs. 'We are starved for variety. The people, no matter how educated – anything tickles their nose they think is champagne.'

Fielding flicks on the tape input and launches into the hard-driving opening of *Eight Days a Week*. He goes through all the chords, getting them right the first time. His fingers dance among the humming copper wires.

Hermann frowns but Fielding feels elated. He decides to celebrate. Precious reserves of cash are dwindling, even considering how much he made in the international bond market of '83; there is not much left. He decides to splurge. He orders an alcoholic vapour and a baked pigeon. Herman is still worried but he eats the mottled pigeon with relish, licking his fingers. The spiced crust snaps crisply. Hermann asks to take the bones home to his family.

'You have drawn the rank-scented many,' Hermann says heavily as the announcer begins his introduction. The air sparkles with anticipation.

'Ah, but they're *my* many,' Fielding says. The applause begins, the background music comes up and Fielding trots out on to the stage, puffing slightly.

'One, two, three –' and he is into it, catching the chords just right, belting out a number from *Magical Mystery Tour*.

He is right, he is on, he is John Lennon just as he always wanted to be. The music picks him up and carries him along. When he finishes, a river of applause bursts over the stage from the vast amphitheatre and Fielding grins crazily to himself. It feels exactly the way he always thought it would. His heart pounds.

He goes directly into a slow ballad from the *Imagine* album to calm them down. He is swimming in the lights and the 3D snouts zoom in and out, bracketing his image from every conceivable direction. At the end of the number somebody yells from the audience. 'You're radiating on all your eigenfrequencies!' And Fielding nods, grins, feels the warmth of it all wash over him.

'Thrilled to the gills,' he says into the microphone.

The crowd chuckles and stirs.

When he does one of the last Lennon numbers, *The Ego-Bird Flies*, the augmented sound sweeps out from the stage and explodes over the audience. Fielding is euphoric. He dances as though someone is firing pistols at his feet.

He does cuts from *Beatles '65*, *Help!*, *Rubber Soul*, *Let It Be* – all with technical backing spliced in from the original tracks, Fielding providing only Lennon's vocals and instrumentals. Classical scholars have pored over the original material, deciding who did which guitar riff, which tenor line was McCartney's, dissecting the works as though they were salamanders under a knife. But Fielding doesn't care, as long as they let him play and sing. He does another number, then another, and finally they must carry him from the stage. It is the happiest moment he has ever known.

'But I don't understand what Boss 30 radio means,' Hermann says.

'Thirty most popular songs.'

'But why today?'

'Me.'

'They call you a "sonic boom sensation" – that is another phrase from your time?'

'Dead on. Fellow is following me around now, picking my brains for details. Part of his thesis, he says.'

'But it is such noise –'

'Why, that's a crock, Hermann. Look, you chaps have such a small population, so bloody few creative people. What do you expect? Anybody with energy and drive can make it in this world. And I come from a time that was dynamic, that really got off.'

'Barbarians at the gates,' Hermann says.

'That's what *Reader's Digest* said, too,' Fielding murmurs.

After one of his concerts in Australia Fielding finds a girl waiting for him outside. He goes home with her – it seems the thing to do, considering – and finds there have been few technical advances, if any, in this field either. It is the standard, ten-toes-up, ten-toes-down position she prefers, nothing unusual, nothing *à la carte*. But he likes her legs, he relishes her beehive hair and heavy mouth. He takes her along; she has nothing else to do.

On an off day, in what is left of India, she takes him to a museum. She shows him the first aeroplane (a Piper Cub), the original manuscript of the great collaboration between Buckminster, Fuller and Hemingway, a delicate print of the *Fifty-Three Stations of the Takaido Road* from Japan.

'Oh yes,' Fielding says. 'We won that war, you know.'

(He should not seem to be more than he is.)

Fielding hopes they don't discover, with all this burrowing in the old records, that he had the original Lennon killed. He argues with himself that it really was necessary. He couldn't possibly cover his story in the future if Lennon kept on living. The historical facts would not jibe. It was hard enough to convince Immortality Incorporated that even someone as rich as Lennon would be able to forge records and change fingerprints – they had checked that to escape the authorities. Well, Fielding thinks, Lennon was no loss by 1988 anyway. It was pure accident that Fielding and Lennon had been born in the same year, but that didn't mean that Fielding couldn't take advantage of the circumstances. He wasn't worth over ten million fixed 1985 dollars for nothing.

At one of his concerts he says to the audience between numbers, 'Don't look back – you'll just see your mistakes.' It sounds like something Lennon would have said. The audience seems to like it.

Press Conference.

'And why did you take a second wife, Mr Lennon, and then a third?' In 2180 (or 2108) divorce is frowned upon. Yoko Ono is still the Beatle nemesis.

Fielding pauses and then says, 'Adultery is the application of democracy to love.' He does not tell them the line is from H. L. Mencken.

He has got used to the women now. 'Just cast them aside like sucked oranges,' Fielding mutters to himself. It is a delicious moment. He had never been very successful with women before, even with all his money.

He strides through the yellow curved streets, walking lightly on the earth. A young girl passes, winks.

Fielding calls after her, 'Sic Transit, Gloria!'

It is his own line, not a copy from Lennon. He feels a heady rush of joy. He is into it, the ideas flash through his mind spontaneously. He is doing Lennon.

Thus, when Hermann comes to tell him that Paul Mc-

Cartney has been revived by the Society for Dissipative Anachronisms, the body discovered in a private vault in England, at first it does not register with Fielding. Lines of postcoital depression flicker across his otherwise untroubled brow. He rolls out of bed and stands watching a wave turn to white foam on the beach at La Jolla. He is in Nanking. It is midnight.

'My old bud, then?' he manages, getting the lilt into the voice still. He adjusts his granny glasses. 'You know, I don't think I'll know how to deal with him. I really don't know.' Something swells up inside him –

And Fielding's world collapses.

The walls fold. Colours drain away, scarlet to pink to grey. Darkness rushes in.

He is watching a blank dark wall, smelling nothing, no tremor through his skin, no wet touch of damp air. Sliding infinite silence. The world is black.

– Flat black, Fielding adds, like we used to say in Liverpool.

– Liverpool? He was never in Liverpool. That was a lie, too –

– And he knows instantly what he is. The truth skewers him.

Hello, you still operable?

Fielding rummages through shards of cold electrical memory and finds himself. He is not Fielding, he is a simulation. He is Fielding Prime.

Hey, you in there. It's me, the real Fielding. Don't worry about security, I'm the only one here.

Fielding Prime feels through his circuits and discovers a way to talk. 'Yes, yes, I hear.'

I made the computer people go away. We can talk.

'I – I see.' Fielding Prime sends out feelers, searching for his sensory receptors. He finds a dim red light and wills it to grow brighter. The image swells and ripples, then forms into a picture of a sour-faced man in his middle fifties. It is Fielding Real.

Ah, Fielding Prime thinks to himself in the metallic vastness, he's older than I am. Maybe making me younger was some sort of self-flattery, either by him or his programmers. But the older man had got someone to work on his face. It was very much like Lennon's but with heavy jowls, a thicker moustache and balding some. The grey sideburns didn't look quite right but perhaps that is the style now.

The McCartney thing, you couldn't handle it.

'I got confused. It never occurred to me there'd be anyone I knew revived. I hadn't a clue what to say.'

Well, no matter. The earlier simulations, the ones before you, they didn't even get that far. I had my men throw in that McCartney thing as a test. Not much chance it would occur, anyway, but I wanted to allow for it.

'Why?'

What? Oh, you don't know, do you? I'm sinking all this money into psychoanalytical computer models so I can see if this plan of mine would work. I mean whether I could cope with the problems and deceive Immortality Incorporated.

Fielding Prime felt a shiver of fear. He needed to stall for time, to think this through. 'Wouldn't it be easier to bribe enough people now? You could have your body frozen and listed as John Lennon from the start.'

No, *their security is too good. I tried that.*

'There's something I noticed,' Fielding Prime said, his mind racing. 'Nobody ever mentioned why I was unfrozen.'

Oh yes, that's right. Minor detail. I'll make a note about that – maybe cancer or congestive heart failure, something that won't be too hard to fix up within a few decades.

'Do you want it that soon? There would still be a lot of people who knew Lennon.'

Oh, that's a good point. I'll talk to the doctor about it.

'You really care that much about being John Lennon?'

Why, sure. Fielding Real's voice carried a note of surprise. *Don't you feel it too? If you're a true simulation you've got to feel that.*

'I do have a touch of it, yes.'

They took the graphs and traces right out of my subcortical.

'It was great, magnificent. Really a lark. What came through was the music, doing it out. It sweeps up and takes hold of you.'

Yeah, really? Damn, you know, I think it's going to work.

'With more planning –'

Planning, hell. I'm going. Fielding Real's face crinkled with anticipation.

'You're going to need help.'

Hell, that's the whole point of having you, to check it out beforehand. I'll be all alone up there.

'Not if you take me with you.'

Take you? You're just a bunch of germanium and copper.

'Leave me here. Pay for my files and memory to stay active.'

For what?

'Hook me into a news service. Give me access to libraries. When you're unfrozen I can give you backup information and advice as soon as you can reach a terminal. With your money, that wouldn't be too hard. Hell, I could even take care of your money. Do some trading, maybe move your accounts out of countries before they fold up.'

Fielding Real pursed his lips. He thought for a moment and looked shrewdly at the visual receptor. *That sort of makes sense. I could trust your judgement – it's mine, after all. I can believe myself, right? Yes, yes ...*

'You're going to need company.' Fielding Prime says nothing more. Best to stand pat with this hand and not push him too hard.

I think I'll do it. Fielding Real's face brightens. His eyes take on a fanatic gleam. *You and me. I know it's going to work, now!*

Fielding Real burbles on and Fielding Prime listens dutifully to him, making the right responses without effort. After all, he knows the other man's mind. It is easy to manipulate him, to play the game of ice and steel.

Far back, away from where Fielding Real's programmers could sense it, Fielding Prime smiles inwardly (the only way he could). It will be a century, at least. He will sit here monitoring data, input and output, the infinite dance of electrons. Better than death, far better. And there may be new developments, a way to transfer computer constructs to real bodies. Hell, anything could happen.

Boy, it's cost me a fortune to do this. A bundle. Bribing people to keep it secret, shifting the accounts so the Feds wouldn't know – and you cost the most. You're the best simulation ever developed, you realize that? Full consciousness, they say.

'Quite so.'

Let him worry about his money – just so there was some left. The poor simple bastard thought he could trust Fielding Prime. He thought they were the same person. But Fielding Prime had played the chords, smelled the future, lived a vivid life of his own. He was older, wiser. He had felt the love of the crowd wash over him, been at the focal point of time. To him Fielding Real was just somebody else, and all his knife-sharp instincts could come to bear.

How was it? What was it like? I can see how you responded by running your tapes for a few sigmas. But I can't order a complete scan without wiping your personality matrix. Can't you tell me? How did it feel?

Fielding Prime tells him something, anything, whatever

will keep the older man's attention. He speaks of ample-thighed girls, of being at the centre of it all.

Did you really? God!

Fielding Prime spins him a tale.

He is running cool and smooth. He is radiating on all his eigenfrequences. *Ah* and *ah*.

Yes, that is a good idea. After Fielding Real is gone, his accountants will suddenly discover a large sum left for scientific research into man-machine linkages. With a century to work, Fielding Prime can find a way out of this computer prison. He can become somebody else.

Not Lennon, no. He owed that much to Fielding Real.

Anyway, he had already lived through that. The Beatles' music was quite all right, but doing it once had made it seem less enticing. Hermann was right. The music was too simple-minded, it lacked depth.

He is ready for something more. He has access to information storage, tapes consultant help from outside all the libraries of the planet. He will study. He will train. In a century he can be anything. Ah, he will echo down the infinite reeling halls of time.

John Lennon, hell. He will become Wolfgang Amadeus Mozart.

Recommended Reading - 1975

Gregory Benford: 'White Creatures', *New Dimensions* 5.
Gregory and James Benford: 'John of the Apocalypse', *Tomorrow Today*.
Michael Bishop: 'Rogue Tomato', *New Dimensions* 5.
Jorge Luis Borges: 'Utopia of a Tired Man', *The New Yorker*, 14 April, 1975.
Edward Bryant: 'Brain Terminal', *Vertex*, August 1975. 'Sharking Down', *Vertex*, February 1975.
Suzette Haden Elgin: 'Babyzap', *Playgirl*, September 1975.
David Ely: 'Always Home', *Playboy*, August 1975.
Nicholas Fisk: 'Find the Lady', *New Dimensions* 5.
Joe Haldeman: 'Anniversary Project', *Analog*, October 1975.
Richard A. Lupoff: 'Saltzman's Madness', *Future Corruption*.
Barry N. Malzberg: 'A Galaxy Called Rome', *Fantasy and Science Fiction*, July 1975.
George R. R. Martin: '... For One Single Yesterday', *Epoch*.
Michael Moorcock: 'Ancient Shadows', *New Worlds* 9.
Larry Niven: 'Arm', *Epoch*.
Patrick Henry Prentice: 'Moonball', *Galaxy*, September 1975.
Bob Shaw: 'Unfaithful Recording', *Analog*, December 1975.
John Varley 'The Black Hole Passes', *Fantasy and Science Fiction*, June 1975.
Joan D. Vinge: *'Mother and Child'*, *Orbit* 16.

Some other Peacocks

Stamboul Train

Graham Greene

Romance, intrigue, espionage, revolution – as the Orient Express steamed across Europe from Ostend to Constantinople (Istanbul) it became for three brief days a world on its own, and within its luxurious compartments the passengers met, mingled and parted, their lives touched briefly though deeply and even tragically by these chance encounters.

Basketball Game

Julius Lester

'I had a visitor today.'
'Who?'
'Rebecca's father.'
'What did he want?'
'He claimed that somebody called him and said they saw Rebecca walking down the street with a coloured boy. And he figures it was you. Was it?'

Allen started to lie, but changed his mind. He was sure his father knew the truth. 'Yes, sir.'

The Disappearance of Odile

Georges Simenon

'Around him there were five million human beings and he was looking for only one, a young girl who did not want to be found, who was perhaps already dead.'

Bob Pointer's sister, Odile, had disappeared from home, leaving behind a threat of suicide. This is the story of his desperate search through Paris in the hope that he will be able to find her before it's too late.

The Ghost on the Hill

John Gordon

'When you go back to university,' she said, 'what will you tell them about us?'

'I shall tell them of your sophistication, of course... You are sophisticated because you all appear so calm... There is more going on under the surface here than in any place I have ever been.'

And Ralph was right. He didn't realize then what effect he and his mother had had on the quiet East Anglian village of her childhood, or that they would act as the catalyst that eased the slumbering tensions and finally released the ghost on the hill.

More fiction in Peacocks

A Bad Lot and Other Stories *Brian Glanville*
The Bad Seed *William March*
The Blinder *Barry Hines*
Bonjour Tristesse *Francoise Sagan*
The Catcher in the Rye *J. D. Salinger*
Cobbler's Dream *Monica Dickens*
Duffy's Rocks *Edward Fenton*
First Love *Ivan Turgenev*
Fly West *Ivan Southall*
Girl with Green Eyes *Edna O'Brien*
The Golden Ocean *Patrick O'Brian*
Good-Night, Prof, Love *John Rowe Townsend*
The House on the Brink *John Gordon*
I Capture the Castle *Dodie Smith*
The Millstone *Margaret Drabble*
Nightfrights *ed. Peter Haining*
Noah's Castle *John Rowe Townsend*
One More River *Lynne Reid Banks*
Only a Game? *Eamon Dunphy*
Parveen *Anne Mehdevi*
A Patch of Blue *Elizabeth Kata*
The Peacock Spring *Rumer Godden*
Ride a Wild Pony *James Aldridge*
Shane and Other Stories *Jack Schaefer*
The Son of Someone Famous *M. E. Kerr*
The Summer After the Funeral *Jane Gardam*
True Grit *Charles Portis*
Walkabout *James Vance Marshall*

... and Non-Fiction

Bird Count *Humphrey Dobinson*
Chance, Luck and Destiny *Peter Dickinson*
Conservation Scene *Geoffrey Young*
The Endless Steppe *Esther Hautzig*
Finding Fossils *Roger Hamilton*
Help! *Barbara Paterson*
I Can Jump Puddles *Alan Marshall*
King of the Barbareens *Janet Hitchman*
Overkill *John Cox*
Motorcycling Book *John Dyson*
Signs of Life *Ian Ridpath*
The Rambling Soldier *Roy Palmer*
Travel on the Cheap *Jonathan Walters*